Paper Music

Wayne H.W Wolfson

To Roscoe Mitchell

CONTENTS

Forward   i

Pattern Recognition: The New York School of Painting & Morton   1
Feldman

Going to Museums   49

Totem Thoughts: Mendelsohn & Goethe   57

In Service of Beauty: D'Indy & The Schola Cantorum   77

Italian River Flows   95

Paris Prints: Gericault & Idem Paris   109

House of Poets: Russian Classical Music   149

FORWARD

Once again, I take up what I hope will be akin to an amusing and informative conversation with people whom I mostly will never meet.

With this, my second collection of essays, I have grown more familiar and comfortable with working in the genre.

Indirectly, technology played a part in how I conceptualized the pieces. We are living through generation blog. It is a time when strong opinion seems to be readily accepted in lieu of actual facts, regardless of the subject. My essays are not meant to be scholarly treatises but I did go to great lengths in my overall research.

My main goal is still to present ideas and knowledge in such a way as if the reader is hearing an interesting chat.

We all make totems, especially with art, of the things which speak to us. This is natural. I try to never speak in absolutes where things are subjective. I also steer clear of placing my agenda and perception within the context of discussing an artist's place in history.

On the other hand, it is justifiable to call a specific work of an artist important in comparison to others in their oeuvre. That is not to say a "minor" work may not move someone more. I always leave room for that possibility in my assessments.

A good essay may not just inform on a subject one is already interested in but also potentially introduce other things connected, which one had not even been aware of.

This happened to me often over the course of my research. I came across then new discoveries of artists and works which I now hold dear.

With a little luck, this book will now do the same for you.

W. Wolfson July, 2017

PATTERN RECOGNITION: THE NEW YORK SCHOOL OF PAINTING & MORTON FELDMAN

There exists an old Persian legend: There was a bug who spent his entire life in the world's most beautifully designed Persian rug. All the bug ever saw in his lifetime was his problems. They stood up all around him. He couldn't see over the top of them, and he had to fight his way through these tufts of wool in the rug to find some crumbs somebody had spilled on the rug. The tragedy of the story of the bug in the rug was this: that he lived and he died in the world's most beautifully designed rug, but he never once knew that he spent his life in something which had a pattern.

I gladly agreed to make the meeting by train instead of flying. The money not spent on plane fare by the gallery was thus not thought about and so did not call attention to itself, discretely slipping back into my fee. For the past few years I had been doing mainly 9x12" works which easily fit in the red leather folio Ottorino had given me one birthday, so my comfort as I sat in my chair watching the landscape slide by was not intruded upon by a pile of canvas transport tubes.

There was always a reluctance to leave my arrondissement but I knew that I must fight through it. It was not so much being away from home but the logistics of getting there which bothered me, although the train was less traumatic than flying. It was this slightly lesser apprehension which allowed me to steel my resolve merely by telling myself that I had to once again get out in the world in order to counter the risk of only ever painting my female friends and the same rooftops bristling with their terracotta chimneys.

There are some collectors with no real passion behind their acquisitions. Even while merely being driven by speculating on a market whose rules were slightly more abstracted than those of the Bourse, a few managed to steadily make money. While building up their commodities they also sometimes accumulated a respectable collection. Their checkbooks gave them entrée into the gallery world and we all had to give of our time to them occasionally as if they had an eye for anything besides the fluctuating numbers.

I would rather make sales for less money to novice collectors with smaller bank accounts but bigger passion. As noble as this sounds though, I knew it was an impossibility since this would most likely trap me at a set level for my entire career. Older and wiser, I now no longer tie myself up in knots about the purity of motive on the part of who buys my work. In my more jaded moments as I shrug to myself I imagine that conceivably some of my current collectors would end up buying my works from the younger more passionate ones anyways, and at a steep discount when they became too hard up for cash for life's basic necessities.

I have always been too clever for my own good, a quick turn of mind which accommodated me by providing articulation to justify anything. I was feeling lazy. I told myself that it was because I was about to let go with a flurry of activity and this need for stillness was merely the calm before the storm. I could easily make the train back home. I could afford to stay the night, to celebrate my sales letting myself fall face down into a giant bucket of mussels while doing quick sketches in-between refilling my bowl as to be able to empty the zinc pail but not so fast as to distress myself. My slightly extended stay would serve as a sort of penance for my mature-self's indifference to the nature of some of my collectors and the fact that I already had in my head by way of justification the sentence;

"Yes, but collectors are not the same as an audience."

I had left my arrondissement but had the time away been long enough for me to get something out of it?

There were plenty of rooms at my preferred place which was close to the Gare de Bruxelles-Central and would allow for an early departure in the morning. I could conceivably be back in Paris the next day quick enough to not have a headache from going without a coffee immediately upon waking.

Transferring my pocket pad to my coat, I leave my book bag on the bureau and head out. Past the Grande Place the tourists and daytrip sightseers drop away. My eyes flit to the buildings with their interesting filigrees and art deco flourishes, I could be in Vienna, or some of the smaller side streets on the Right Bank. On the rare occasions when I found myself there I would stop to look at the better preserved specimens of a bygone era where Proust once bought his silk pocket squares, now turned into luxury boutiques manned by politely indifferent staff. Here, these buildings are not unified in their aesthetic, which allows for the sensation of wandering through a familiar but non-specific European city.

I find myself in a more lived in area occupied by locals or so it seems after the near artificiality brought on by the museum like aspects of the guide book destinations. Pretty gilded dead things give way to smaller cafes where people are eating salads and no one has a map. I do not know what I want and so order a coffee which I do not desire, to bide my time and form a more cohesive plan.

I drink it too fast which is all right as it was not that well-made and so not worth savoring. I put my money on the table and leave, the speed of my stay marking me as a tourist but the fact that I left a tip lending itself to doubt.

The kapellekerk, as old as it is there is not as much ostentation as can be found on some of its peers. I had found my way here by complete happenstance. I am not particularly fascinated by churches but as I was right here, I decided to go in. I vaguely recalled some point of interest, perhaps the relic of some saint I had once taken a fancy to after doing some reading?

There was no one around, not even the volunteers one usually encounters in such places who quietly sit in corners making sure all remains well. My eyes drifted around, there was dust which diffused the light coming in through the stained-glass windows, painting the elongated stone saints which hugged the pillars in soft hues of yellow and blues.

I saw the heavy bronze plaque which denoted the spot that Pieter Bruegel rested. This was the thing which had opaquely been stuck in the back of my mind. There were tarnished brass stands with their slotted halos to which velvet ropes were attached. They were red but seriously dust-graying at the temples and not even extending all the way across to block the alcove off from all the tourists who never came.

Since there was no one there to stop me, I took a tentative step behind the rope, moving closer to what remained of the master. I stood there for a moment, years of struggles and triumphs that I had faced flashed through my mind, not coherent scenes but rather the emotions, mercurial, good to bad and back again. I drank in the plaque a moment longer, nodded to myself and said out loud;

"Yes, I too only want to do good work."

I left putting a few Euros in the donation box which was otherwise empty.

Now present was a hunger which was legitimate and not merely an activity to stave off boredom. The barkers all along Petite Rue des Boucher stand in front of their restaurants and as if from the tower of babel, shout out their places charms in various languages. All the menus are similar with chalkboards leaning against the walls next to the doors offering up the days specials, the first inevitably being moules et frites. Many of the restaurants have canopies which color the immediate areas under them in a lighter shaded version of their plastic skin. Some of the better places have what look like long rectangular marble topped sinks, minus their faucets, which are filled with ice and piled high with what seafood they have to offer. Rose trout, sea bream and snapper wear diadem of ice flakes.

I sit down at one of the places which does not seem as busy but other than the number of tables occupied, no different than the rest. I position myself at what would be "my table" were I back home at one of my usual haunts. It was now, among this steady stream of people, some filling up the tables around me, that I felt alone and a little bad. Now, I had gotten what I needed before going home. Happy to be blue, I took out my pocket pad and began capturing all around me as I waited for my meal.

I find myself second in line to get a ticket for the first train back. So much of Europe is connected and easily traveled by train. Yet when departing, each country has its own distinct characteristic. The ticket warned to be on the platform a minute before departure. I am in my seat settling in fifteen minutes before. I look at my watch, the minute and hour hand are at exact position of us leaving. Before I can finish my thought, which was a sort of inner sigh at what will most likely be a five to ten-minute delay the train shoots forward with no fanfare. Not that I had expected a brass band but the casual yet timely manner in which the Brussels trains depart always surprises me.

A woman in a uniform of the same color scheme as that of the conductor comes by pushing the type of trolley as that which one gets their food off of on a plane. It is very early but out of automatic habit she gives me the full list of beverages'

"Vin, Coffee, thé…"

She blushes slightly at having made mention of the wine this early.

I ask for tea but then after thinking for a moment nod at the wine with my chin.

"Les deux."

After being handed my cup. Glass and bottle, a basket with various pastries and rolls are held out to me. I take a napkin and randomly grab what turns out to be a crusty roll. She smiles, smooth's out her skirt against her thigh with her palm and continues on.

I drink the tea first since I would rather have the tea alter the taste of the wine than vice versa. The countryside slides by, I watch a million landscape paintings move in the opposite direction. I lean back and relax into the steady motion towards home. I wish I had an older brother who had died seven days before I was born. That way I would always have had someone watching out for me. Instead I find that I am the older brother…

I get home and shave, accompanied by some Coleman Hawkins. I feel not a new direction but a new series, the idea slowly percolating. Walking around the art store might shake it free and if not, I still need to get some blenders and erasers.

There were a few hours to kill before the stores opened. My sense of etiquette prevented me from arriving anyplace right as they were opening their doors as I understood the importance of wanting to get settled in as to start a work day smoothly.

I went to The Rostand. Standing at the bar it was not the early morning workers whom I sometimes shared a coffee and calvados with at my regular bar but it was still locals and not the sightseers that would largely commander the patio later.

I strolled around the Luxembourg. I had preferred paths and decided to do some which were equally as good but not my usual route. Past the pétanque courts I take a left to bring me back towards the main gate. The plane trees path, a leaf haze green canopy that shimmers when swayed by the breeze. Resentful, as its beauty goes largely unnoticed.

Walking through the store I envision pieces which while utilizing the density that I prefer, only use a limited palette of black, white and pink against a gray background. Before committing to canvas, I will play around with paper. A small pad of gray paper and colored pencils whose twins I probably already own.

Since I get a discount anyways, I would rather spend the money than find out I am wrong than have to go back out again to stock up. Even with the erasers the bag is small and I do not bother sticking it in my book bag.

On a subconscious level, I think I want to carry the bag for the little pulsations of pleasure it gives me, tangible evidence of being so far removed from the past when I had to budget out ahead of time even the smallest purchase.

Passing a café, I am waved down by Helene. I sit down to join her for a drink. Some acquaintances of hers from London happen by and also sit down to join us which was a stroke of good luck for me, as I could not immediately remember if I had been in the dog house with her again or not.

I do not even remember how it had come up. It was too early for drunken revelry so partially inspired by the shadow of the pantheon looming over us, someone got the ball rolling on pseudo deep talk. Not used to drinking before dinner, Stewart with flushed cheeks told of having been sure of taking some class prize as a child, coveting the little lead fob that was given to the winner only to see it go to a classmate who had gone the entire semester largely unnoticed by all but a few of his classmates.

Exhaling with a bemused smile he leaned back in his chair;

"And, what was an important moment in your early years?"

Instinctively my index finger slipped under the space between two shirt buttons and touched the scar in the same manner that religious person would their saint medallion.

"I do not think in such terms…"

Before I could get annoyed or the tension became ratcheted up, Helene waved the waitress over for another round. Nostalgia was the misstep that she could ill afford and so she understood me. Helene had the timing of a musician. Pointing her index finger straight up, she made it do a circular motion to the waitress who left with three nods of her head.

She went to squeeze my hand but knew that I was sensitive about them being touched and so just let finger tips delicately brush my knuckles.

"Well, I can tell you, for me it was when I met Doc…"

She had kept the peace and as a bonus had managed to surprise me. The whole thing was quickly forgotten as the waitress returned with our drinks.

Stewart looked at the table for a moment through his wine glass. He watched me add the water to my pastis.

"Ugh, I do not know how you can drink that beastly stuff, it's so strong."

"Wine before dinner, especially vin rouge and in this heat, you will not even manage to stay awake until dinner..."

Finally, Stewart's group took their leave. Helene and I now floated upon a sea of varying sized empty glasses. I had to go to the market, she invited herself which I did not truly mind.

The Port Royal market. Tables piled high with bouquets of flowers. Sprays of color, fireworks with trailing verdant tails which hold them back from infinity. It took me a moment to realize that she was putting all the ingredients in my bag to make Palermo sauce. She had been watching me; waiting for me to realize what she was doing. Once I noticed she clasped her hands together in front of her, right over left, wrists touching and silent movie star batted her eyes at me.

"OK."

Dinner had worked its magic being so good that we both ate more and quicker than we should have. While the dishes soaked Helene decided to take a bath.

"Come keep me company."

The heat from cooking had not been too bad and was dissipating. This curtailed the need to take a walk which was good as I wanted to, if not start working outright then do some reading to help inspire. Helene drew a bath. As I was poking through my records I heard her call me in to chat. I grabbed one of the many pads I always had lying about.

She had been too impatient to let the tub fill completely before getting in and so a trickle continued to descend from the spout. Her hands both with soap bubble barnacles pushed her hair back so that I could better see her face.

Even with the lid down I just could not bring myself to sit on the toilet in front of her and to use the lip of the tub would change the perspective so I sat on the floor with my back against the door using the robe which hung from the hook as padding.

I quickly executed a series of drawings each which emphasized an emotional truth of the moment. I was pleased with them all but it was the last one which pointed me in the direction I would take for my next series. The hot water had cause a condensation on the wall above the tub. The beads would swell then some would run down already established paths leaving odd shaped dry patches so that it all became a land surveyor's map of river veined country. The dry sections created almost a negative space which gave the pattern of the wall a depth. I wanted to incorporate more pattern into my work but not as artifice such as occurred in the oeuvre of Klimt but the way as organically encountered in the everyday.

The dawn had softly whispered something to me. I glance over at her. Still, she sleeps deep in color fields, two blankets of different hues the top one folded down to her knees. Since they could not make their minds up, one of the cats stayed in bed to absorb the warmth of the sheets while the other followed me into the kitchen to witness the ritual of my coffee preparation.

I would like to put some music on but both Helene and my neighbors would be effected by the too thin walls through which Bach would leak. I turn on the stovetop, gas hissing its hello. The cheap white bowl, part of a set that we had bought at the China Faire. The bottom of the bowl, greyish silver scratch marks from her lucky spoon and the ghosts of a thousand café cremes.

While I wait for the coffee to brew I let my gaze go out the window. If one were to stare at the sides of the buildings which also faced into the shared courtyard, after a while it is easy to at will reduce them down to a series of flat planes of off white, weak coffee brown and starfish pink. To further Mondrian it, every few windows have a painted wooden box with geraniums which are metamorphosed into a series of Morse code dashes.

From amongst these dashes at both dawn and dusk comes the distinctive cry of a bird. Maybe year after year it is not literally the same one but regardless when not here, I often hear that call in my dreams.

I poured the coffee out into two cups to cool, curious to see if she would remember which she considered her lucky cup. There was nothing left to do and I felt that there were not too many legitimate complaints that she could make for me kicking her out of bed.

Helene had started trying to awake on her own accord. She now lay on top of the sheets thinking the discomfort of the cold air would force her into motion but she remained in a drowse. I stood at the end of the bed looking at her.

Looking at if someone had started sweeping the floor but having left off before finishing, there was a thin line of dark hair that went from below her naval down to her sex. I leaned down towards her. My pulse ran backwards, the dishonesty of desire. Had she asked me which dress she should wear, I would not merely shrug my shoulders as occurred in my head.

Always the blue one.

I was distracted by desire but also fueled by it. I usually liked to get an earlier start than I had today but I felt the next series percolating. I sensed it almost ready to be born full formed. This temporary schedule worked to Helene's advantage and so she had the good grace not to complain when upon finishing our coffee and toast I put the dishes in the sink by way of cueing her that the time for departure was imminent.

I did some of my best thinking while taking a bath or walking. I had to go see my framer, Marc and knew that the circuit via St. Germain des Prés would be the final incubation period needed for the series conceptualization.

I walked Helene to the metro. I was going to make a little small talk as to not have my meditative silence misconstrued for regret but I could not remember what her work situation was although I know that I should have.

We embraced at the top of the stairs, she leaned back, looked me in the eyes and squeezed my hands while saying;

"See you around Kid."

Marc and I had always worked well together. He usually did a good job and for a discount since I let him place a small emblem on the back of the frame with his shop's name on it. Our association had the veneer of friendship but the same could be said to exist between myself and all the bartenders who regularly poured for me. It was just my code of conduct, polite and gracious until messed with.

Our dynamics and the fact that his girlfriend ended up becoming pregnant by another while they were on one of their temporary "breaks" combined to make him not concentrate as hard on his work. A businessman on vacation wanted to buy some Paris art, whatever that meant. His catch was that he wanted the pieces to be small enough to fit in his luggage and not take up too much room. I think jazz played in too large a venue loses its power and paintings under a certain size seem still birthed. His size requirement put off a lot of my peers who shared my point of view.

I offered up some 5x7" graphite drawings. We talked over drinks which had loosened his tongue. He told me that he did not know about buying merely drawings as he was worried people would not realize it was art bought in Paris;

"I need the awe of overseas bought art and for it not to seem as if merely a framed print or possibly something carefully cut out of a magazine."

Despite being a tourist, he was immediately embarrassed after having permitted the wine to lubricate his throat which allowed said sentiment to escape. I told him my feelings on small paintings. This perked him up as he felt like he was getting an inside track.

"Do all painters feel this way?"

I told him that aside from myself a goodly number of my pals did. He stroked his chin with the blunt end of his thumb while thinking. Wanting to make up for his faux pas and planning on checking out more paintings but wanting to have a backup plan should all painters feel the same way, he agreed. I normally did not rush to fill conversational silence but during the contemplative lull that fell upon the table I reassured him.

"Framed up, you and everyone back home will instantly know that it is art."

We shook and I used a ballpoint pen to do a napkin map of some of the better places to eat and drink on my side of the river.

Marc had not completely dropped the ball and untrained eyes may not have even noticed but to me, the frames did not work in harmony with my pieces as much as they usually did. I told him that I would never begrudge him not being able to take on a job for whatever reason, so long as I had warning to allow me to line up an alternative framer. There would be no hard feelings and I would return with more work for him on the next job.

Although a little nervous, I could tell by the look in his eyes that we understood each other, the whole dressing down taking far less time than I had anticipated. We parted with a handshake.

I decided to take long way back, meandering through St. Germain des Prés. I stop for a drink near where Apollinaire used to live. I noticed how the crowds sort of merge into one gelatinous animal then break apart becoming smaller and smaller at every traffic light only to grow again a little further down the street. The patterns of life transfix me, being receptive to seeing them allows for all things to become grist for my mill.

I have usual tables all over the city. I took my usual table in the far-left corner. It afforded me not only a view of the entire bar but also the sidewalk as well.

Walking so briskly as to almost be at a run, the florist late, one arm through a white flowered wreath which rested upon his shoulder. He would have looked like a lifeguard had it not been for his dark suit.

There is an older couple sitting in the booth towards the back. Neither moves, not even a little. If they blink, then they manage to do so when no one is looking. They seem unaware of even each other's presence. Shoulders starting at the top of the green leather upholstered booth back, their shadows stay close to them equally as to the door; only ever able to merely bare mute witness, a fate unfair since they manage to maintain year in year out thicker outlines than their flesh counterparts.

I decide to use the placemat for my doodles. Like my hand upon the page, I let my mind wander. The drink and pencil cause everything else to drop away. I can examine anything from the safety of the preoccupation of my raison d'être. It is not always weighty matters though.

For no particular reason, my mind pulls out one night another lifetime ago. Kit and I had thrown a small party. Less a soirée than a group of people with minimum wage jobs pooling what little extra money we had to do a pot luck and buy a few large bottles of stock alcohol.

People began to trickle away. I helped with the dishes because I knew that if I didn't they could very well be left in the sink indefinitely. Seeing them there again upon my next visit would be oddly demoralizing. I forget how it came up but as we finished, the fact that she always confused Jules Verne and George Orwell was mentioned.

There was no one left but she and I, her cousin from Poland snoring away on the pile of clothes waiting to be put away in the bedroom.

"Orwell wrote *Animal Farm*…"

"Then what did Jules Verne write?"

"*The Time Machine*."

She scrunched up her face as she would later do more frequently when she eventually needed glasses or was doing math.

"No, I am pretty sure that was H.G Wells."

There was the small ghost of a drink left in the bottle. She took some and passed it to me confident that my laziness in not wanting to wash nor retrieve more glasses would prevent me from complaining.

In my head, I started reciting the names of all the Jules Verne books that I could think of. We both lay back on the couch doing and saying nothing. It was in this way I had figured out how to become immortal. I sat forward now slightly more alert which served to wake her up a little as she thought I was rallying myself to make some criticisms on her friends not all of whom I liked.

13

I told her that I figured out how one could become immortal but that it involved time travel. If one went into the past and died, you would still be born again in the future. She pointed out to me that the downside to this was that the traveler would live forever but within a very specific loop and they would not be aware of being in the loop so it would be an immortal within a Mobius strip. All of that aside there is no time traveling, if they invent it in the future we would have it now as at least a few tourists in any given location always break the rules.

It became so late that our talk began to lag, voices sounding muffled by the thickness of encroaching sleep. I had the solution for immortality but quickly lost it. It would not involve time travel but patterns. It was deceptively simple but my conscious mind cannot quite do the recall. If one said;

"Thursday I am going to go to the bank."

And linked onto that a sentence, something along the lines of having just gotten back from the bank.

I might have half dreamed this solution. Once in a while I try to recall it. Sometimes I imagine coming up with it again as an old man. Surprising everyone in the neighborhood by being around decades down the line and none too worse for the wear. The only thing of it I have retained was that it was a pattern of words connected to an activity which they described.

As I work on the delicate shading of the woman off to my left's eyelashes I hum a little to myself. I am by no means a good technical singer but I think I sound better singing than humming. Perhaps because as on a subconscious level I feel it more dignified. I softly switch to words, idly for myself become overly aware that someone may hear me, try to switch to words for the tune which I have forgotten and so split the difference with a sort of vocalese. I get, if not the lyrics then the cadence and pattern right.

Patterns can serve as both device and delivery system for the emotional intent of a piece of art. Especially in the mediums of music and painting.

I used to say women were my biggest source of inspiration, their beauty, their mystery. It seemed such a painterly thing to say. That though would be exhausting, as it would not allow full exploration of possibilities in any artistic medium since that kind of thing calls for a certain degree of retreating to within oneself. Something which is rarely appreciated or understood by those not actively doing their own explorations. Beauty wants to be acknowledged not patiently wait on the sidelines to be taken out for a night on the town.

Now, I am not bashful about saying my main source is music. Music too has its magic encoded in patterns. To understand these patterns does not payoff in some impossible gift but rather the receiving of an emotional resonance as intended by the composer.

I had cut my musical teeth on the romantic era works. I knew the history and importance of the post romantic era composers but the components of discordance where their artistic antecedents might have used a swell or in less subtle hands, some bombast, turned me off.

My music collection had some of the essential works of the usual suspects of modernity, Schoenberg, Stravinsky et al. I had done a lot of reading on both composer's lives and the theories behind their compositional technique. It all seemed like something I would gravitate towards but my initial listening left me cold. I would move on exploring other works, slowly moving outward from the prerequisite of the composers having sprung from the romantic era.

I have so much music that once a day I randomly grab an album off the shelf to sort of break things up listening habit wise. Mixed in with this practice, I would occasionally go back to revisit those works which had left me indifferent.

After many years of exploration, on one of my random listens the music cliqued. I got into Schoenberg first although even now with a knowledge and affection for his work I must be in the mood to listen to it. I do feel the same can be said though for most work of substance in general.

The newfound appreciation enlarged the scope of my explorations and led me to other composers and connections that made sense in my mind at least, to new painters. Once one is into an artist and is more than passingly familiar with their works, no matter how radical they may seem, there is to be detected in different proportions elements from previous generations.

Arguably it could be said that Stravinsky and Schoenberg are the two fountainheads of Western modern classical music. Their influence has trickled down through the generations, sometimes if only serving as a jumping off point for technique which they empowered by providing something that was both still relatively new and to be rejected as yet newer ways are sought.

Schoenberg's seemingly unique genius, compositionally unorthodoxy, had traceable precedents in aspects of what some of the late romantic era composers were doing. His early works were more closely connected in their cadence, rhythm and to a varying degree, structure than what he would go on to create. He would make a radical departure, developing his own compositional systems but they evolved organically from the components of his artistic forefathers. New patterns built from and off of old. Notes hanging in the air like impasto swatches of color, mirroring their power to move one's soul.

It is the same with American painting. The great loose knit New York school of the 1940's was dubbed "Abstract Expressionists" by Robert Coates in 1946. The term had first been used in 1919 in a German magazine *Der Strum* for German Expressionism which encompassed not just painting by the mediums of architecture and cinema. In the United States, critic and theorists Alfred Barr used it in 1929 for German painter Wassily Kandinsky.

The most influential of the New York school most affiliated with the moniker was the trio of Willem de Kooning (1904-1997), Jackson Pollock (1912-1956) and Arshile Gorky (1904-48).

All three had the foundation of formal training. Of equal importance to their foundation was the crosscurrent of inspiration and liberation. The inspiration was not as structured nor formalized as, for example, Cubism had been. A revolution where it becomes a sort of template with exacting compositional layouts and subject matter that's created a very specific lexicon (playing cards, instruments et al). This effect birthed a different type of formalism that eventually became limiting even to Pablo Picasso (1881-1973) and George Braque (1882-1963), the genres progenitors.

In New York, even with how different what each painter was doing from one another was, theirs was a departure unified in how they used momentum of earlier generation(s) to push off from.

For the New York school, it was more a case of one artist coaxing another to challenge themselves and the established ways, many of which had actually once been the radical innovations of the then young lions. The goal was to not forge a new school but for each to achieve an overall freedom both personal and artistic.

Germany and Austria had made important contributions to Modernism, serving as incubating grounds for new genres of the plastic arts with The Viennese Secessionists and in Germany Der Blaue Reiter group. Although the later included non-Germanic painter/theorists Russian Wassily Kandinsky and American Albert Bloch neither of these countries were the places burgeoning painters aspired to make the pilgrimage to.

The capital of modern art in the first half of the 20th century was Paris. The "it" neighborhood changed over the decades as the artists migrated from one to the next. From Montmartre to Montparnasse then spreading out to Saint Germain de Prés and The Latin Quarter.

The main appeal was inexpensive places to live and work. The attraction of other artists being around became a factor after the beachhead having been established. The things which make an area appealing for working artists also carry within them the seeds of their own ruin. Once an area is known to be conducive for painting, more and more artists arrive. There becomes a shortage of space so that landlords can raise the rent negating the all-important cost factor. The sense of community becomes soured by the appearance of curiosity seekers and hanger-on which makes working uninterrupted harder.

There was still much important art being made in Europe but after

World War II the focus began to shift overseas to the New York school. In looking back, there was no lynchpin moment when the focus shifted nor one sole reason.

Part of the catalyst could have been that there had been so much innovation occurring with rapid succession over the past half a century that while not everything was fully or instantly accepted neither did it feel completely fresh. The war changed so much morally, intellectually and spiritually that new art was called for in the new post war age. This new art needed to be radically different as any nostalgia via technical connection to what had previously come in art would feel either sadly faux or shamefully naïve.

As people began putting their lives back together in post war Europe, unless one were an actual artist, au current theory and innovation in the plastic arts would seem to be of a least important concern. Also in the zeitgeist would be the dichotomy of obeying the urge to examine what had happened while also trying to temporarily forget as to begin to move on.

Stateside artists gravitated towards New York City for many of the same reasons that specific neighborhoods of Paris held popularity. The possibility of living on the cheap and the comradery of one's peers aside, another reason which was not as much a factor in Europe was a general acceptance for the artists if not of what they did then their presence. America, especially in the years immediately leading up to the Eisenhower era could never be misconstrued as a bastion of free thought and intellectual exploration but New York did possess more willingness to enfold intellectuals and bohemians into its urban tapestry than most of the rest of the country.

With its skyscrapers a visual shorthand for the modernity of a new age, some of the old-world artists thought of it with apprehension akin to the sailors weary of sea serpents and sailing off of the edge of the earth.

It was this perceived remoteness which, during the rise of dictators and turmoil of the war, made America seem a far safer bet than a country which could be trained to for artists fleeing fascism. Arriving from overseas, New York was easier to get to than most other places in the country save for maybe the active San Francisco port. If America though seemed remote, then the west coast was even more so. The arrival of older exiled generation of modernists in New York would be a much needed ingredient towards a forming of an American Modernism.

There was no wide acceptance of modern art but it had started to make inroads into the publics conscious with the 1913 Armory Show which encompassed what was going on in America (often by artists who had gone abroad and soaked up some overseas modernism) along with diverse genres from throughout Europe in multi disciplines.

There were not many large galleries or modern art dealers with an understanding which went past what comprised their own limited tastes. In 1924 Pierre Matisse, youngest son of the French painter opened his first gallery, in New York. His was a well-developed eye that combined with a keen understanding of many of his father's peers and those he inspired. It can never be overstated the importance that he played in bringing European modern art to America.

Well before the war Pierre Matisse had been working to facilitate a market for the modern art. His presence and efforts would have also added appeal to New York for European artist going into exile.

The germination period of the mid-thirties saw modern American painting start to truly forge its own identity. There would still be traceable elements of post Impressionistic ideas from Europe but this would be combined with a new world aesthetic.

"The Ten" (1936) was the first of a series of loose knit groups which formed in New York that encompassed a new burgeoning artistic sensibility from which would spring multi genres of painting.

Depending upon who was interviewed and in what year, the reason for the group's initial formation is debated. One of the agreed upon main reasons was as a direct response to protest the lack of attention and respect due American abstract arts by The Whitney Museum. The members of the group did not all share common artistic touchstones but had similar philosophy of emotions over any concrete pictorial narrative. At the time of the group's formation only member Ilya Bolotowsky, inspired by Mondrian, was fully non-objective and abstracted although fellow member Marc Rothko was heading in that direction in his own way.

A year later the group would splinter, with a new one "The American Abstract Artist" being formed by Mondrian acolyte, Harry Holtzman. Members of AAA and The Ten would talk in bars, cafeterias and diners, willingly including nonmembers in their discussions.

Mondrian and Kandinsky were the two biggest proponents of moving away from representational painting. Paul Klee was a direct contemporary of Kandinsky, both having been members of The Blue Rider Group and teachers at the Bauhaus school. Although they both drew on music and shared similar theories, Paul Klee's was a more personal journey. The lessons which he learned, eventually projecting outwards to the benefit of others, whereas Kandinsky included more of an intentional and immediate constant putting forth of theory in how he worked. The audience/peers were in a less passive position in the equation.

Mondrian and Kandinsky would inspire with teaching, essays, lectures and talks. Both combined non-painterly ideas into key components of their artistic philosophy. Mondrian choosing a theosophical bent, relating the creative act to a journey to spiritual purity and attained knowledge. While Kandinsky linked much of his inspiration to music, claiming "Music is the ultimate teacher."

The two painters had many differences in both technique and philosophy but shared a commonality in wanting to liberate painting from nature and the traditional pictorial narrative. Kandinsky, a major theorist of modern painting, put down many key ideas to his work in a series of essays. One of his most important essays was "On the Spiritual in Art" (1910, English trans 1914).

Previously, elements of a break from pictorial narrative had been found in the works of a handful of painters; Joan Miro, Yves Tanguy, Kazimir Malevich. All of them had a style/technique but not a proselytized system. Kandinsky further articulated the mission of a new art which included biomorphic shapes, abstracted lines and color ruling over coherent forms in a painting;

"Color in itself free of cohesive form and visual description of things can conjure and resonate emotions."

This would be a reoccurring theme enlarged upon by the New York School. Much like a piece of music such as jazz or a passacaglia this theme would be executed with countless variations among The New York School.

All of these factors further combined in 1935 during the Works Progress Administration program (1935-43). This was a new deal program created by President Franklin D Roosevelt to provide jobs while also positively effecting neighborhoods. Artists were employed for mural and other public art projects along with regular painting and activities tied into their disciplines. Exiled European artist such as Fernand Léger were employed working side by side with their younger New York counter parts in endeavors both artistic and menial.

This was the first time American artists came together in such large numbers to devote themselves fully to art. By 1936 six thousand plus had joined. These numbers gave each individual confidence as it made them feel as if no one was trying to break the mold alone.

Founding member of AAA, Harry Holtzman helped Mondrian flee Europe to America in 1940. Mondrian would disseminate his non-pictorial theories while interacting with younger New York artists. His presence being a further totem of artistic liberation for The New York School to feed off of.

Hans Hofmann was another mentor like figure. In the first decades of the century he had studied in Paris. He had big eyes not limiting himself to merely one school but taking what he found worthwhile from Matisse, Cubism, Kandinsky and Klee. This unfettered approach empowered all those in New York to whom he lectured and gave his time to via long informal chats. Not being bound by any one school there was no limit to the scope of exploration in technique. Hofmann's umbrella theory under which everything else fell was the importance of a "grammar of painting". The essence of this was that a painting's importance and meaning not needing to derive from its subject matter. It was an art for art's sake where technique and emotional intention of the work overwrote the traditional importance of programmatic subject matter. A lynchpin concept for the abstract expressionists and many of the sub genres which evolved out of them leading right up to pop art which like to some extent Surrealism before it emphasized concept and near totemic images. Kandinsky, Mondrian and Hofmann all very different as men and artists but all preaching a break from the pictorial at the same time to the same group of receptive artists.

For the New York School, bolstering the freedom found in this concept and their interactions with older exiled European peers was their empowerment found amongst themselves. The cafeterias, studio parties and bars substituted for the rich café scene of their Parisian counterparts.

The style most associated with abstract expressionism to the more causal art fan would be the work of Jackson Pollock from the late 40's until the early 50's, even though his would be more accurately be put in the genres of Total Painting or Action Painting.

If the paintings created during the apex of his career were a cathartic wail, then it occurred with a jazz like spontaneity as there was no philosophic or aesthetic objective behind it but merely a few traceable influences (Wolfgang Paalen, Janet Sobel) and some later imagined ones originating from theorists' minds.

There exists now a commonality between Picasso and Jackson Pollock in regards to (general) public perception. In his first few decades in Paris, Picasso's great inventiveness was a call to arms for new ways to regard the creating of art. It was the reason he was such an important North Star for so many painters who would become greats in their own right. As modern art got more adherents, it then became his protean activity that held appeal as a touchstone.

These legitimate points of admiration have dropped away. Now even people who do not know art, know who Picasso is. He is admired by a whole new generation of artists and would be/want to be's. Even in non-painterly disciplines he is an artistic zenith to be striven for. This has nothing to do with his earlier compelling points though.

It is because Picasso has become a sort of shorthand for one doing what they want, especially bad behavior, and being applauded and maybe even thanked for it. The popular image of Picasso gobbling up women regardless of their other attachments then going into a bar and running up an exorbitant tab which is then settled by a single napkin scribble. His fecundity and longevity are no longer the point. The reality of the amount of daily solitary studio time put in would turn away many of the aspirants.

Jackson Pollock's image has become a similar if not quite as large a touchstone. He too gives off the vague whiff of freedom to do what one wants. His well-known drip paintings give the "anyone can do that" type of feeling. In the modern era's obsession with being famous for doing nothing, the appeal is work which takes no work. The images that have come down to us of Jackson Pollock working in his barn studio insinuate that at most a little theater must be given while making the drips. Think what you want of these paintings, he did have years of formal foundation under him before finding his identifiable style.

Although I know it was work, I am not a fan of his paintings. For me it is not a case of feeling "money for nothing" or even "the emperor has no clothes". In retrospect, his works power had the shock of the new. There is a density but with no intellect behind it, the viewer is left to do all the work. Now down the corridor of time, it is the once young lion grown docile and fat off of zoo supplied steaks.

There was not often the acrimony and feuds among The New York School as so often bubbled up with their European counterparts over technique or aesthetics. This is partially because aside from the pursuing of freedom and artistic evolution there was no formalized prerequisites to which their works had to submit in technique nor subject matter. What terminal feuds would bubble up later would largely be resentment over fees and usually involved only the concerned parties and not any kind of group or city-wide schism.

All the painters would break off into smaller groups but still socialize, certain artist's orbits intersecting with several circles at once. Culturally, an artistic freedom was obtained. American painting had forged its own identity. The pursuit for freedom could now be put aside for one of personal evolution. The overall philosophy of emotion's importance over representational elements in a work would largely remain the soul of most artists work for their entire lives. Some would dabble or add traditional elements such as in Willem de Kooning's Women series. Even when the occasional traditional aspect showed up it would now vibrate with a freedom from the past.

People have forgotten how to look at paintings. It is resultant largely from the fact we all now have the ability to instantly capture photos or movies any time or place often at the expense of living in the moment.

If one draws a portrait it must be hyper real or close to it to be appreciated. Yet more often than not when looking at any hyper realistic drawing, one marvels at the technical prowess but the work does not travel outside the gallery or museum with the viewer, in their head.

I have known artists far better than myself but the hyper realism lends a coldness to the work, a flatness to which no emotion can cling. In these cases, they would have been better served being "looser" in some way.

When Matisse paints a woman laying on a couch, the viewer knows what they are seeing. The foot looks like a foot although far from realistic. One is aware of looking at a painting. Yet there is a joy which still powerfully emanates from his works decades after both artist and model are in the ground. Matisse was figurative but used color to convey emotions. The colors were not in service to the subject but collaborating with it.

In 1949 one of The New York School's strongest theorist, Mark Rothko admitted to being into Matisse's *Red Studio* which was then showing at MOMA. He credited it as a key source to his use of color as power unto itself. With the freedom that came with his burgeoning fame, Rothko traveled to Italy in 1950. He was influenced by the frescoes of Fra Angelico (1395-1455). Fra Angelico mostly used soft colors which seemed to almost throb. Their softness has an organic component which lends itself to this effect as opposed to the rich lushness of Titian (1488-1576 *The Sun Amidst the Stars*)

For Rothko, in the early 40's there was an influence from the Surrealists of utilizing a lexicon of symbols mined from the subconscious.

As was the case with a lot of his evolutions, this was bolstered by his reading. In this case that of Jung, Freud, Joyce and Thomas Mann. His work from this period shows him more directly descended stylistically to his immediate European predecessors who utilized biomorphic abstractions (Tanguy, Miro etc.) than what he would evolve into. As he sought emotional power for work freed up from the need of concrete subject another prime influence was Nietzsche's *The Birth of Tragedy out of the Spirit of Music* (1871). Simply put, it states that that the human condition as put forth in Greek tragedy and myths were universal and perennial. Life in Greek times was not a golden age but rife with conflicting emotions of the two impetuses behind human behavior, Dionysian and Apollonian. This dichotomy was part of an intellectual and emotional struggle which made up civilization.

Rothko would name pieces after classic tragedies. The pieces were not meant to be programmatic, reflecting specific scenes from a work but to mirror the overall feel of its namesake while also echoing what was going on in the chaotic here and now of the war years, the reoccurring echo of the Greeks and mankind. A savage piece should not put forth merely visual representation of a specific time or event but the universal feeling ever occurring down the corridors of time.

He would shed this aesthetic by the end of the decade as he pursued greater emotional clarity and intensity with works that made no direct reference to subject matter outside of color being the emotional delivery system.

Clement Greenburg, an early champion of The New York School, when writing about Mondrian said;

"Mondrian didn't aim at perfection, it (the works) aimed at nothing outside of itself."

This art for art's sake, rejecting need of any power deriving from subject matter was in line with the scope of Rothko's ambitions. It was combined with his own brilliance and the possibilities of colors emotional power bereft of program as gleamed by among other things his absorption of inspiration via Matisse and Fra Angelico.

Later he would seek a further concentration of emotion by having his works untethered even by the loose restriction of title, substituting in numbers (*No 31/No 13, No 61*, et al).

Throughout his early career Rothko insisted that he was not an abstractionist. The works which he is best known for, the squares of color are often termed "multiforms" even though Rothko himself never used the label.

The multiforms are indicative of the artistic phase he would spend the rest of his life in although from their initial conception and execution in the late forties, they would be further perfected. An important factor to these paintings is their obvious liberation from any sort of representational images. It is not merely the colors he chooses for these paintings which give them their power but how the paint was applied. Much like Mondrian's Lozenge Series (1920's), the way in which the paint is applied is also important. Rothko utilized various materials as to allow for dense layers of coloring which also had a luminescent delicacy.

With the multiform works, a specific distance the viewer should stand from the work (18 inches) and height from the ground where often in his mind. Most of the multiforms are on the larger side. They are freed up from philosophy and psychology offering up a free form spirituality. The effect of both color and technique especially with the richer colored ones (blues & reds) is powerful. The smaller squares seem to be floating in the larger square of the canvas. There is a shimmering along the edges of the smaller squares so that it could be either glowing cubes slowly pushing through a viscous liquid of the main canvas or a sort of portal whose edges are aglow as it waits for something to come or go.

As the years went on Rothko, always the great theorist, felt misunderstood even in the midst of his financially rewarding fame. There was the frustration of words now not being adequate to the task of describing what he was trying for with his work.

Rothko took pains to avoid labels for himself and his work. Technically his work could fall into several categories which were soon birthed after The New York School gained wider recognition past its own adherents. Lyrical Abstraction, Color Field and Minimalism all contain elements of what Rothko as doing although not necessarily inspired by him.

Barnett Newman (1905-1970) was a direct contemporary of Rothko. He is categorized in with the abstract expressionists mainly from his association more than his work's aesthetic. A commonality was that his work did break from the figurative and previously established painterly traditions. It would be more accurate though to describe his genre as color field. There were two ways in which he drastically differed from Rothko whose multiforms his work cursorily resembled. Unlike Rothko, the technique of application was a steadfast flat application of color which eschewed expressive brushwork. Also, Barnett added titles to his work which while not necessarily visually apparent, gave the pieces specific program as opposed to Rothko's unfettered free emotivism.

Barnett Newman's flat, bright surfaces without variation would serve as an inspiration to Frank Stella (1936). Frank Stella in the late fifties was doing paintings which were a continuation of keeping out the traditional pictorial forms. He continued the tradition of color field genre but also the emotional coolness of Barnett Newman's work. Like Barnett he would also give meaningful titles to his works which gave each piece specific meaning.

Frank Stella's work in the fifties with its emotional detachment helped popularize the genre of Minimalism which can be said to be the cerebral child of Abstract Expressionism and Color Field painting. Minimalism in its earliest phase incorporated the waning influence of abstract expressionists' aesthetics and philosophy.

Frank Stella would give some works titles which were as important as the work's technique, being a component of the piece's meaning. The late fifties Black Painting series being emblematic of this. *Die Fahne Hoch* (1959) was ironically named after the first line of The Horst Wessel Lied which was the anthem for The National Socialist Worker's Party. This use of satirical irony was a throwback to the Dadaist and Surrealists and would also figure large in many pop art movement pieces. Another connection to Surrealists and Dadaist was the lightly buried multiple layer of meanings.

Frank Stella used the same proportions as that of the party's official banner by way of trying to further subvert their power and ownership of things. The first line in English is "Raise the banner". There is the symbolism of a flag being raised to proclaim himself on the scene and a new branch of painting while also providing a tip of the hat to Jasper Johns whose painting *Flag* (1954-55) he was familiar with.

Frank Stella's philosophy was that of a picture as an object, not something from nature nor the artist's psyche. This totemic approach would be very much in line with Jasper Johns (1930) and Robert Rauschenberg (1925-2008). Specific meaning would once again figure as a component of painting and sculpture supplanting the spirit of what the abstract expressionists had striven for.

Jaspar Johns and Robert Rauschenberg would figure as sort of evolutionary link between what had come before them and the burgeoning Pop Art movement. More than The New York School the two of them would draw upon the distilled inspiration of previous generation's French theorist/artist Marcel Duchamp (1887-1968).

It is often reckoned that next to Picasso, Duchamp is the most influential artist of the 20th century. In some ways, this is an accurate assessment as aspects of his theories remained in practice and an inspiration across mediums decade after decade crossing continents.

The degree his theories remained in the fore over the years varied but never completely disappeared. Duchamp came from a traditional painting foundation but at a time when the norm was revolutionary (nascent cubism). He wanted to free his work from the painting tradition and also maintain his personal freedom by avoiding working from within a group. Over the course of his life many groups tried to formally claim him as a member and while he would interact with them he always remained intentionally man on the outside, free from having to follow even revolutionary rules.

In 1915, he started the first of many trips to New York. Eventually he would get a place in Greenwich Village (1942) and become a U.S citizen (1955). By the time that he started his major travels he was well on his way to rejecting traditional canvas painting and sculpture.

Once he rejected painting, the importance of Duchamp's art lay in its philosophy. Concept is a major factor to many of his works even when not provided to the viewer. The question of intent often shares equal importance as it also raises the question of what constitutes a work of art. This was a type of freedom as it allowed for no limits to how emotion and message of the artist could be conveyed. Even with elements of chance in a work though, there was always a concrete program via concept.

Duchamp's philosophy of the role of intent and its questioning of what is art is typified by his deeply influential Ready Mades. The first one he created was in 1914 and simply titled *Bottle Rack*. This was a metal rack with prongs upon which washed wine bottle would be stuck to dry. It was a factory made common everyday object which became art by him dubbing it so. Before the Ready Mades, there had been work leading up to the concept such as his *Bicycle Wheel* (1913). While the bicycle wheel was a common object he did alter it with intent by nailing it atop a wooden stool as to be able to spin the wheel. Since not anyone could buy such a thing prefabricated it did not meet with the concept of the Ready Mades. Once he clarified in his mind the concept of Ready Mades there would be no major alterations to an object.

Concept as component was important to the work and theories of Duchamp's work as was layer of meaning and often a wry sense of humor. In 1919, he began doing "assisted Ready Mades" the most famous being the piece *L.H.O.O.Q.* This was a cheap postcard of the Mona Lisa onto which he drew a curved Poirot moustache and pointed beard along with the letters on the bottom margin. The name of the piece is play of French pronunciation "Elle a chaud au cul" which has to do with a sexual restlessness and heat.

Robert Rauschenberg's Combines can easily be seen as the offspring of the Ready Mades. Works like *Bed* (1955) and *Monogram* (1955-59) used non-artistic, found objects which then would be combined with more traditional artistic mediums such as paint to create art. Like Duchamp there were also often multiple meanings to the works which came from intent and also the artist's own personal mythos.

Jasper Johns often used contrasts in his early works, expressive painting of commonplace items or subject matter which harkens to the spirit of dichotomy in Duchamp's Ready Mades. His mix of high and low, visually referencing what was then in the American zeitgeist shows Johns as an immediate precursor to the Pop Art movement. Another commonality with Duchamp is a subtle, at times satirical sense of humor. The humor and mix of high and low is something else that would be embraced by Pop artists, from the comic book kitsch of Roy Lichtenstein (1923-97) and Andy Warhol's (1928-87) mundane made emotionally stilted but glamorous works.

Duchamp would have no influence on the first wave of abstract expressionists or The New York School in general. His shadow would fall over the next generation. Conception as component, personal iconography and humor being important to the Pop artists' going right up to today from Claus Oldenburg to Jeff Koontz and Damien Hirst.

While the main progenitors of The New York School would not have any real influence on the next generations of painting they did influence other mediums such as the poetry of Frank O'Hara (1926-66) and composer Morton Feldman (1926-87).

Both Morton's work and life would be intimately entwined with The New York School. He would continue to create long after the movement gave way to others. New York at that moment in time is the only place which could have served as a hothouse to nurture such a diversity of artists who all shared the commonalty of pursuing various forms of freedom. Morton, utilizing a different medium, fit right in.

His parents were Russian immigrants. Morton's father was initially the foreman for his uncle's garment factory in Manhattan before he started his own garment factory which manufactured children's coats.

At the age of nine (1935) Morton began to compose his first pieces. He was enrolled at the Third Street Settlement School on the lower East Side of Manhattan. After three years of study he was taught by Madame Vera Maurina-Press.

She was the daughter of a well off Russian attorney. She had been friends with visionary pianist/composer Alexander Scriabin. In Germany, she studied under Ferruccio Busoni. She founded The Russian Trio with her husband and brother in law. At the outbreak of World War ii she had to flee Germany, arriving in New York via Brazil.

In New York she took up teaching gifted children for a low fee at the Chatham Square Music School on the Lower East Side.

Madame Press was not rigid in curriculum, allowing for exploration and each student to find their own voice. It was while studying with her that, by his own admission, Morton would start thinking about "a certain type of tone" which would factor into his compositional style.

When he was fourteen, money was tight. His father was still only a foreman at this time. Thrift was called for on the part of the whole family. Keeping up on his studies, Morton found that the family piano was no longer adequate for his needs.

To a certain degree, there was resentment on the part of his father as he had never had time himself for intellectual pursuits. Morton's maternal grandmother who lived with the family fostered his voracious reading and burgeoning autodidactic intellectualism.

By way of continuing to show her support, Morton's mother had him go to the Steinway House to pick out a piano. Ideas of "tone" were already coalescing in his nascent sense of compositional aesthetics. His mother did not offer to accompany him and with no help from the staff he picked out his own piano with what he described as an "absolutely singular tone". All of his free time was spent at the piano until it was practically an extension of himself.

Morton was fortunate that New York received such an influx or artist and thinkers emigrating from Europe. Via the actual artist or their first generation of students, it allowed for him to build a foundation which eschewed the dogma of tradition and the equally system based avant-garde.

The second of his important teachers was Wallingford Riegger (1885-1961) with whom he took up studies in 1941. Wallingford was the first American composer to use a form of Arnold Schoenberg's twelve-tone system. He did not rigidly abide by the system for all his compositions and when Morton at the age of fifteen took private compositional lessons from him, he completely eschewed passing on the system in favor of more traditional counterpoint tasks. As with Madame Press it was a continuation of foundation accompanied by an exploratory freedom.

In 1944, after high school, Morton registered for the entrance exams for New York University. He showed up on the day of the exams with his older brother. He made it as far as the examination hall where the sight of all the other candidates made him feel certain that it was not the path that he was meant to take.

Throughout his life, Morton would always be weary and occasionally contemptuous of academic composers. He felt that as they composed largely only for those within their orbit that it became more about a work's construction and the theory behind it than the music's inherent emotional properties.

In lieu of attending university, he would work at the family's business for the next twenty-six years, taking great pains to not proclaim himself a composer.

Like his painter counterparts, Morton had a traditional (formal) foundation. The manner in which he pursued it though was more akin to that of an autodidactic. He benefited from the way his teachers chose to teach him. Each in their own method of incorporating the freedom for him to find his own voice.

An immediate effect of this was that unlike a lot of his peers in both music and painting he emerged on the scene almost fully formed in regard to aesthetic identity. There would be components of his work such as the duration of a piece or constructional methodology like using graphic notation, which would change or be dropped. There was never though any radical sea change from one phase to the next over the course of his career.

After having given up lessons with both Madame Press and Riegger, Morton spent some time retreating into his art. In 1944 a friend from high school who was also a composer was recommended by New York Philharmonic conductor Dimitri Mitropoulos to in exile German composer Stefan Wolpe as a student.

Due to personality differences, the composer declined to take on the student. After introducing himself to Wolpe, Morton was taken on as a student.

Stefan Wolpe (1902-1972) was born in Berlin. He had a progressive formal music education, studying under Ferruccio Busoni, Franz Schreker and at The Bauhaus school. In his early work Stefan studied and utilized the second Viennese school progenitor Arnold Schoenberg's twelve-tone system. He was also very involved with workers' rights and various socialist and communist groups for whom he wrote songs.

Just as Morton later would lean towards an anti-academia stance for music, Stefan wanted to avoid the feeling of talking down to or over the workers' heads with his songs. For these pieces, he worked in different sonic vernaculars of the day than his other work, incorporating populist elements such as jazz. To his delight, all these songs would be sung and enjoyed by his intended audience.

With the rise of the Nazi Party, Stefan was in twice the danger for being both Jewish and an avowed communist. Unaware of how much worse things were about to come, he traveled through Romania and Russia ending up in Austria in 1933.

He spent a year studying under one of the other main composers of the Second Viennese School, Anton Webern. When the socio-political climate in Austria became hostile, Stefan again had to flee. He emigrated to Palestine, where he would remain for four years.

While in Palestine teaching at the conservatoire, he wrote songs for the communal farms. These pieces were similar to the workers' songs he had been writing in Europe. Concurrently he was also composing works in the style of the second Viennese school.

These pieces were felt to be unpalatable, the immediate effect being that his teaching contract was then not renewed for the following year. Wanting unrestricted artistic possibilities, Stefan and his wife wanted to emigrate. Safety from the terrors of fascism was as equal a factor as that of artistic freedom which made New York City the natural choice.

Stefan's wife, Hilda Morley (1916-1998) came from a family of artists and political activists. She had been born in New York but at the age of fifteen moved to Haifa, Palestine. Her formative years would be spent going to school at the University of London. She would correspond with and meet older established authors William Butler Yeats and H.D Doolittle. German bombing of the city was the catalyst behind her return to New York in 1940.

Through her second husband, the painter Eugene Morley, she became enmeshed in the New York School. Even after her divorce she remained an active participant on the scene.

Hilda would go back to Palestine, returning to New York yet again, this time with Stefan, her third husband. It would be through her in the early fifties that he would be introduced to the loose knit New York School of painters, composers and authors.

Stefan acted for Morton in a similar fashion as that of Hans Hoffman had played to the New York School's painters. He brought with him not a rigid, specific system but aspects of European modernism unfettered by being of only one way of thinking.

The ambient environs of New York added to Stefan's own palette even as he was freeing up younger composers. His teaching, at least with Morton, was more to instill a sense of freedom than provide any compositional method or aural template.

After the fact Morton often described his lessons as a series of long talks. As Stefan had no compositional system to push, Morton said that he gave the gift of allowing him to find himself organically.

Stefan was important to Morton but they often did not see eye to eye. A testament though to Stefan's importance was the fact that they would remain in touch long after Morton artistically came into his own.

An inspiration with whom Morton had the briefest interaction was then in exile French composer Edgard Varèse (1883-1965). Varèse was seen by Morton as an alternative to either of the twin wellsprings of modern classical, Stravinsky and Schoenberg.

As Morton was taught by Stefan and as he would later use in his own teaching, Varèse was less about a system and more about an overall philosophy towards composing. The philosophy providing a goal to work towards in a composition but the manner of which one achieved it being open ended, free of a one-way system.

Timbre was an important aspect of Varèse's composing as was rhythm. Morton said that he only had "one lesson, on the street with Varèse. It lasted half a minute, it made me an orchestrator."

Varèse told Morton to keep in mind the amount of time that it takes the music to go from the stage out into the audience.

In Varèse's own compositions he would often fragment and rearrange patterns. He talked of sound as "living matter" and "musical space" as open rather than bound. He had two inspirations that went towards formulating ideas for fragmented sound. The first was architectural and fed into his idea of space and time being factors for music. Listening to Beethoven's "Seventh Symphony" at Salle Pleyal in Paris he noticed during the scherzo section that the sound broke up due to the venues architecture and in its dissolution from what it had originally been, transformed as it floated away. This effect would be incorporated into his work.

Another touchstone was the writings of philosopher-mathematician Jozef Wronski (1776-1853). He put forth the idea that music was the "corporealization of intelligence that is in sound". Morton would use his own take on this in his works.

Just as the painters Rauschenberg and Johns had sought to make a painting not a representational object of something else but a thing unto itself, Morton would work to incorporate silences not as an effect/device but as an integrated part of the whole, working not for but with the overall mood and sound. The importance of timbre whether solo piano or orchestra/ensemble was also influenced by this idea.

Aside from Wolpe the other important figure during Morton's artistic nascence was John Cage (1912-1992). Cage was born of eccentric parents in Los Angeles. His father was a tinkerer whose works were often interesting but impractical. While his mother was an occasional journalist for the Los Angeles Times.

While studying theology at Pomona College (CA) in 1928 he became familiar with the works of Marcel Duchamp. Feeling that there was faulty methodology to how the university taught, he decided to leave after a year.

With his parents help, he would spend a little over a year in Europe as to find himself via a calling.

He started in Paris, trying his hand initially at architectural studies. Painting and writing were also attempted. It was while in Europe he discovered the modern music of Stravinsky and Paul Hindemith (1895-1963) but also baroque master Johann Bach.

Even with his new revelations, he wanted to go home but his parents talked him into further exploring Europe.

His wanderings took him though France, Germany, Capri, Spain and Majorca. This was where he wrote his first musical composition. For this maiden piece, he used nontraditional notation that incorporated math instead of notes.

Although not happy with the actual piece, it was a start. Spain was also important to him for an experience he had with ambient sound which was like a variation on Varèse's at the Beethoven concert.

While out on a walk all the ambient cacophony of individual activities floated up into the air to create a singular new unified one.

In 1931, he returned to Santa Monica, California where shades of Duchamp, he made a living by advising collectors and museums on what to buy and lecturing on modern art.

At this time, he had his first music teacher, Richard Buhlig (1880-1952). By 1933 he decided to focus his energies solely on composition, dropping painting.

Some letters were written to composer/pianist Henry Cowell (1897-1965). Cowell would sometimes employ unorthodox ways of playing the piano, such as forgoing the use of its keys for manipulating the strings directly. This technique would later often be employed by Cage in his own compositions for what he termed "prepared piano".

Cowell seemed reluctant to offer Cage any direct help but did suggest that he take up studies with Schoenberg. He went on further to suggest that Cage might want to strengthen certain parts of his foundation by first studying under former Schoenberg student Adolph Weiss (1891-1971).

This facilitated the need to move in 1933 to New York. Initially once on the east coast he paid his bills by becoming a wall washer at the Y.W.C.A.

He studied with Weiss while also attending The New School. Between work and academics Cage had a grueling schedule which only allowed for four hours of sleep a night.

The intensity with which he threw himself into his studies allowed him to be ready to approach Schoenberg in under a year. Unfortunately, he could not afford the cost of Schoenberg's fees. Asked whether he was willing to devote his life to music, so emphatically did Cage say yes that Schoenberg waived his fee.

Cage studied privately with him as well as at University of Southern California and after that UCLA. Schoenberg became a lifelong inspiration for Cage whose influence never waned.

Sculpture/collage artist Xenia-Andreyevna-Kashevaroff (1913-1995) married Cage in 1936. One of the many jobs that he took during this time was as an accompanist for dance classes at U.C.L.A. While playing these traditional programs of music he was also experimenting with using scraps of metal and found objects as instruments, inspired by a discussion with proto-multimedia artist Oskar Fischinger (1900-67) whose mystical theory was that everything in the world had a spirit that could be released via sound. Mysticism aside, it made sense to Cage that anything could be made to work in the service of music.

Using a curriculum similar to what he had experienced at U.C.L.A he began teaching at Mills College in 1938. Having already experienced aspects of the dance world as an accompanist, he began to work with dance troupes and choreographers in conjunction with his own work. With a deepening interest in dance, after only four months at Mills College he moved to Seattle to work with choreographer Bonnie Bird at the Cornish College of the Arts.

Simultaneous with his duties at Cornish he and Lou Harrison (1917-2003) formed a touring percussion ensemble which got him his first notice. This was also the start of his first forays into utilizing prepared piano which bolstered his rising reputation.

Cage desired to create a center for experimental music. He had a similar belief to Varèse that non-instrumental sounds could also easily be put into the service of music. Also like Varèse he foresaw a future where technology would introduce electronic equipment that would allow for easy ways to compose and produce music with new sounds.

He accepted an offer in 1941 from the painter Lazlo Moholy Nagy to teach at the Chicago School of Design. Cage taught and once again worked as an accompanist but no opportunities for his center arose.

His rising reputation did land him a commission from Columbia Broadcasting System to compose a soundtrack for a radio play, *The City Wears a Slouch Hat* by poet Kenneth Patchen (1911-72). Cage saw the commission for if not a start towards parlaying the exposure towards establishing his center, then at the very least an opportunity to utilize the thus far unavailable to him equipment he had dreamed of for the score.

The conception for the score was to forgo traditional instrumentation, instead using sound effects to make the music. The text used sounds as means of description throughout the work and the protagonist was merely referred to as "The Voice"; so it would seem that his concept would perfectly mesh.

Cage wrote 250 pages of descriptive score after being told by the studio's sound engineer that "anything was possible".

The score was turned in a week before the performance. Immediately he was told that his imaginative score was unplayable. Swallowing down his disappointment, in one week he composed a far more traditional score for percussive instruments that minimally incorporated some amplified sound effects.

The music which was performed and its subsequent parlay power were far from matching up with Cage's initial conception. Of small consolation were a few positive letters about the piece which were sent to the station.

Having met heiress, and up and coming gallerist, Peggy Guggenheim and her then husband, artist Max Ernst, they got along so well that Peggy extended an invitation to stay with them when in New York.

Feeling that the project, although it had not been what he had envisioned, could still serve as entrée to bigger things, Cage spent the last of his money on bus tickets to New York. Once there, Cage and his wife stayed with Peggy and Max. She facilitated his introduction to Marcel Duchamp, Piet Mondrian and Virgil Thompson.

Peggy started planning for a concert of his music for her new gallery. On his own initiative, he set up a concert for the Museum of Modern Art. He also planned to take on more score work at Columbia's New York office.

Arriving at the Columbia offices, to his embarrassment, he discovered that the score had not been considered a success and that they had no desire to ever work with him again. Peggy viewed MoMa as rivals and his plans for a concert there as a betrayal. She refused to pay for the shipping of his instruments from Chicago and kicked Cage and his wife out of her home.

Without the availability of his percussive instruments, he had to fall back upon the easier to utilize prepared piano for which he began to write some of his most important works. Feeling alienated from a lot of his peers and down in general, he began a study of Zen and Eastern Philosophy.

From his trials a new aesthetic was emerging which drew from his recent studies. Added to this was inspiration from reading a copy of the I-Ching whose chanced based mechanics he began to incorporate into compositions in 1950. Random chance had been a component in some of his earlier work but it would now rise to the fore.

Carnegie Hall had a program of Webern and Rachmaninoff. After the first part, Webern's "Symphony op 21", Morton was annoyed by the disrespect that the audience showed the work. He decided to leave early.

In the lobby, he met John Cage. Morton had known him by sight but the two had never actually met. By way of introduction, Morton approached his fellow composer and said;

"Wasn't that beautiful?"

They talked and made plans to meet.

Cage threw a party at which Morton was introduced to many luminaries of the New York School, including his soon to be best friend, the painter Phillip Guston (1913-80).

Cage provided Morton with introduction into the upper echelons of the New York bohemian art world. From the start of their friendship, stylistically the two had little in common.

Morton never tried to minimize Cage's importance to his development which was more spiritual than technical. According to Morton, Cage gave him the strength and inspiration via observing how he lived, to be himself.

Morton would move in to the apartment below that of Cage's, the building quickly becoming a Mecca for all the artists of the era.

Despite no longer being as artistically isolated and with a growing sense of his own mission, Morton continued to work during the day at his father's coat factory and uncle's dry cleaners.

Just as Mark Rothko was about the emotions of his works being unfettered by the confines of subject, program and later, titles Morton pursued a similar type of purity in his own way.

He would always be anti-system as he felt that working within a specific mode became just another type of framework in which the music became confined regardless of its newness. Morton loathed academic composers too. He felt that in their intellectual freedom, that they were composing only for one another and that their seeking out and utilizing of new theories was a trap in itself.

Cage at this time had begun using elements of chance in his compositions, inspired by and employing the *I-Ching*. Soon he thought of chance elements too as merely another device. If one left space within a piece for chance operations, then regardless of what happened it was not truly random.

Morton's art would have different phases but there were never any radical departures ala Stravinsky. For Morton, it was not so much an evolution as a constant honing of his skills as to be better able to artistically convey what he wanted to say.

In his early compositions Morton worked in "graphic notation" rather than traditional musical notation. The idea behind this was not about spontaneity but allowing the music to remain free from the trap of process.

Graph notation abandons the typical note and stave structure replacing it with various symbols to substitute for the notes.

By Morton's own account, he and Cage spent five years going every night to the Cedar Bar which was the epicenter of modern American painting to participate in the community.

Morton was inspired by painters. He would with his compositions, think in terms of surface. His desire was for music to have a physicality to it akin to what his visual peers were achieving.

In Morton's early graph work, certain elements of the music would intentionally be left out. For example, time may be given but not pitch or pitch but not tempo. Visually, the scores could be works of art unto themselves, ordered abstractions of squares and dots. On a few occasions, Cage would recopy Morton's scores in his far neater hand.

The two composers might mention to one another what they were working on but more often than not their conversations turned towards painting.

Surface for Morton was time. Time though was not the medium in which his work lived in or was built with but one part of the work, an organ in the body of the piece. He has referred to his work aptly as "time canvases".

Just as the New York School made painting representational of nothing save itself, Morton's music, even when titled after a friend or peer, was not meant to convey anything outside of the self-contained world that it created and in which it was the sole occupant.

There was a five-year period from 1953-8 where Morton abandoned graph notation as he felt passages which served to link or unite his intent with the musicians' performance were too static. After rectifying the problem in several ways, he would return to notation a year later in a slightly altered form.

By 1970 Morton quit utilizing graphic notation for the more traditional music notation. To the casual listener there is no stylistic jump. Unlike some composers whose oeuvre is large, if one likes Morton's works, then aside from personal preference of favorites piece(s), there is no phase to avoid.

His late pieces often grew in length. The duration of some of the later works gives the listener a further painterly effect. They pull one into their environs. Morton has filled his plain in such a way that the effect is that of waking all around a painting, viewing it from various angles and distances.

There occurs in these late pieces, moments of hushed delicacy. The silences are not voids as can occur in works by other composers though. They are organically working parts of the whole. From these silences notes emerge or softly retreat back.

The building with its magically artistic denizens in which Cage gathered likeminded revolutionaries around him had been dubbed "Bozza's Mansion", named after the landlord.

This group of which Cage was the unofficial leader began to fracture. The composers had been grouped together similarly to their painter counterparts as another medium of The New York School. Like the school's painters, there had not been an overall methodology such as existed with Schoenberg and his followers.

The commonalities had always been that of a generation finding a new way. The initial phase as they sought their way made it easy to alley with each other despite marked differences in style and ambitions.

As each artist found their voice and gained reputation, it became harder to hold the group together. The initial struggles over, slights and differences seemed a bigger deal. Things came to a head when in 1954 Bozza's Mansion was torn down.

Cage and some of the group moved an hour's ride away. Cage would return to the city in the next decade but by then Morton would be living in Buffalo and most of the original group was dead or relocated.

The sense of being in the trenches together and the sense of a type of communal existence would never occur again for this generation of artists. Morton would still interact with his peers as would Cage, who managed to still have a smaller group gravitate around him.

Like some of his compatriots, Morton saw a rise in reputation which allowed for travel. He and Cage had an uneasy truce akin to two super power nations each held in check by the uncertainty of being able to defeat the other. There would be the occasional public airing of dirty laundry but never an acrimonious final break.

In 1972 Morton was given a teaching position in Buffalo at the State University of New York at Buffalo. He refused to teach in a conventional way, adopting an amalgam of how he had been taught with how he had studied. When the teaching position was made into a permanent professorship which he named The Edgard Varese Chair.

After having his chair for a year, he used his power to found The Buffalo Festival. All the composers and musicians from the mansion Bozza years reunite to perform during the inaugural season.

Morton joined a tour of The Creative Associates of the Center of the Creative and Performing Arts in 1976. Part pf the itinerary for this major tour passed through the near east. It was while in Shiraz that he made his first purchase of an oriental rug. Turkish/oriental rugs would become a passion and source of inspiration for him, lasting the rest of his life.

His interest in oriental carpeting can easily be seen as a natural outgrowth of the deep sympathy with which he viewed the New York School and the painterly way that he approached his own compositions.

The repetition of delicate patterns which utilized a field of color to suspend it while also incorporating its own to harmonize or go against the plane could easily be analogous to much of Morton's own work.

During much of his lifetime, Morton's reputation was eclipsed by that of Cage's. Morton was verbose and articulate but did not seem to work the public persona, fostering the cult of personality in the same way as Cage. To some extent, when discussing their works on their own accord minus all the other elements of both composers such as personality, the debate becomes similar to that of Stravinsky versus Schoenberg.

The last decade of his life saw Morton achieving success and recognition which would expand further in the years after his death. He would indulge in his passion in rugs and travel more comfortably. Success with its financial rewards did not however alter his work ethics in the least.

Throughout his career Morton did not think in terms of rebelling against the established norm in his medium. He aimed plenty of his barbs at his revolutionary peers as well. A clue to his ambitions and aesthetic can be had in his stance against the academic composers regardless of how Avant Garde their music may have been.

He felt they only composed for each other, cut off from anything connected to the real world. While he was not seeking to make music for the masses as his teacher Wolpe had before coming to America, there was a desire that compositions have their own lives outside of that of the intellect of the composer.

Morton concerned himself with the realness of each piece. Its life intersecting with that of the place it was performed, time being not just something which held or framed the notes but an interwoven component. The time between each note, time that it takes for the sound to reach the audience, time difference between the lifespan each note every instrument played.

In 1978 Morton had his own version of a crisis of faith. He worried about the validity of music as true art and not mere entertainment. At the phase of his career he was financially secure and with a reputation if not what it should be in the states, then at least blooming in Europe.

If some of his music was viewed as too short which necessitated that it be put on programs with artists with whom he shared a tenuous connection or none at all, he would now dramatically go in the opposite direction.

Giving no practical thought to physical the limitations of musicians, potential performance venues nor an audiences capacity to maintain being engaged, he wrote many longer pieces. Works like his second string quartet lasts five hours, the same with "For Phillip Guston".

The extreme length of some of these late pieces gives them an added power. They create an environment into which any receptive listener must eventually find themselves slipping into. They exist in time and not merely a duration.

There too are pieces during this phase of his work for solo or small groups of instruments which while not marathon in length clear the hour mark.

So undiluted was his compositional vision by this point, that these pieces have an almost time bending property. They possess a similar effect as to be had when looking at a great painting without the distraction of others being present. Has a minute been spent in contemplation or more, many more?

Morton answered his own question collectively with these pieces. They were not something for people to go to for an evening's distraction. They were a thing to go into, occupying the same space as the listener, different aspects of the music's properties revealing themselves only to be sublimated by others like drops of rain hitting a windshield or paint to canvas.

Much of his work had in one way or another been inspired by

painting and then later rugs. The commonalty being patterns. The effect of this is really apparent in the late pieces. Regardless of duration the effect is akin to that of looking at a painting in a gallery from all different distances and angles. The variations allow for different aspects to become more pronounced but only for that moment.

The painter Phillip Guston had a twenty-year friendship with Morton. They were intellectual equals who managed to stay in harmony a surprisingly long time. Even after their break Morton recited the Jewish prayer for the dead at Phillip's funereal.

Mark Rothko, although not as close, was another good friend. Rothko like Morton and Guston, agonized over theory and the validity of what they were doing. Of great importance was his work's place in society, not its exposure but a comprehension of it.

Famously, Rothko accepted a prestigious commission from the Seagrams company. They had a new building on Park Avenue (NYC) in which the luxury restaurant, The Four Seasons was to go. He was given the plumb commission to supply art for the restaurant.

After doing work on the large pieces he did an abrupt about face, feeling offended at the thought of the rich stuffing their faces decadently while surrounded by his work.

Similar to Morton's concerns of music as art once he started to become successful, Rothko worried over whether the advent of high priced sales for his works was mere trend among the rich with a total lack of understanding on their part.

Throughout his oeuvre Morton has works named after people from his life. The pieces are not meant to be sketches in which the attempt is made to capture the subject's personality. It was a way for him to show respect or that he was simpatico.

In 1965 Rothko accepted a commission from industrialists/philanthropists/collectors, John and Dominique de Menil which was in line with his need of the spiritual purity of art. He was to supply site specific works for the building which would eventually be named after him. Rothko rented a large studio on the upper east side as to not only be able to work easier on the large canvas but also see how they worked when placed together. The design went through several architects with Rothko working closely with the final two Howard Barnstone and Eugene Aubry. It took him two years of hard work to complete fourteen paintings, a large three wall triptych and eleven smaller ones.

Located in Texas, The Rothko Chapel was a place he envisioned people could go for quiet contemplation not affiliated with any one specific faith nor philosophy. The power of art mirroring and collaborating with the power of the spirit.

Rothko would commit suicide in 1970 at the age of 67, just a year before the chapel was completed. Morton accepted a commission from the de Menils to write a piece of music to commemorate the painter but also the chapel itself.

Rothko Chapel is the perfect starting point for someone looking to get into Morton's work. It is by no means watered down but in length and cadence will seem closer in line to what the casual listener is used to. The effect of Morton's work is emotional. Unlike some of his peers, one needs no pre-knowledge if compositional technique nor intent to enjoy it. The work has retained all its power, not suffering a loss of potency from an over familiarity as has happened with Mozart's requiem.

The orchestration calls for a mixed chorus, alto and soprano all of whom sing not words but a sort of haunted vocalese, Viola, percussion and celesta. The instruments are not necessarily what are thought of for chamber pieces and so adds to a sort of timelessness. It is modern but more dreamlike than discordant.

Rothko had been very certain and intentional in the colors he chose to use in the chapel paintings. Morton sought to mirror the mood of the paintings while also keeping in mind the building's shape and the effects it would have on the cadence. Above all else he wanted the music to not merely come at the listener but to envelope them but not by mere force alone. With his music as he had so often before done, he wanted to mimic the shadows and shimmer of paintings. There are parts which feel as if a whisper or errant melancholy thought.

This is as close as Morton would ever come to programmatic music. Besides working in the effects of Rothko's paintings, he worked in a nod towards Stravinsky's *Requiem Canticles*. This was Stravinsky's final work and Morton wrote this part on the day of the Russian master's funereal.

There is a deep hushed stillness in this work even when sound patterns unfold. It shares in its poetic gravity similarities with Olivier Messiaen's "Quartet for the End of Time". Both pieces are abstractly programmatic. Messiaen's work is an elegiac place to lament where even a potential final darkness offers if not renewal then the last kiss of terrible beauty. Feldman's work is the place itself.

As in Rothko's work, the audience becomes an active participant as they pull the work into themselves while simultaneously being immersed in the work's self-contained reality. Time was an aspect of surface for Morton not to be constrained. This work crystalizes some of Morton's desires, to not have the time of a piece exist on its own as duration within the confines of concert hall and having nothing to do with the hours before or after the audience leaves.

Like his other works and some of the painters he admired, repeated listenings offer new things to be noticed. It is a landscape-other place the more of which one sees the more they travel it.

I fill my book bag with records. I am giddy with patterns. I go to Pierre's as I know he has a little upright piano in the corner. I want to stick my coffee spoon under its skirt. I want to pound the hell out of it, to softly tickle it so that it sounds like it is revealing my secrets.

It is the hot season now. Initially there is the claustrophobic feeling as the near on triple digits force me to keep the shades in the bedroom drawn. I adapt, quickly becoming used to it, even reading Flaubert while laying atop of the sheets in my seasonal cave.

The slats of the blinds sway ever so slightly. This causes the light which spills in from the street to strobe upon the ceiling. Looking up from her nap the cat watches them.

"Minnowing" she calls these plays of silver without saying so as to keep an afternoon's treasure for herself.

GOING TO MUSEUMS

I had first discovered Soutine via reading a group biography on the painters of his generation. It brought to the fore a feeling that had already been percolating that I was becoming more and more anti-museum.

All art regardless of medium should have a component of contemplation to it, provided by the viewer. The bigger museums had become more about generating money above and beyond what was needed to be done to keep the lights on. This attitude was mirrored in the art market, where works were treated as high priced commodities, stripped of their connection to any of their intended spiritual or intellectual intent.

People going to Europe for their "trip of a lifetime" have always had checklists of must see; The Impressionists, *Mona Lisa* et al. Everything in the digital age has become accelerated and in this new-found speed, memories and impressions of having seen these works stick in one's mind at best like bugs upon a windshield of a highway cruising vehicle.

Go to the Musée de Orsay or The Louvre and works that have been reproduced countless times in postcards, posters etc. have an endless stream of tourists who run up, do a quick pose as a photo is snapped and then just as quickly disappear.

In the interim, while others wait to flash a peace sign or to make a duckbill face while standing sideways in front of a van Gough, there is the audible hum of people discussing where to go to eat or what is next on the itinerary.

After reading about Soutine and many of his peers easily came the realization that the spirit and conditions in which the paintings had initially existed were so far removed from where they were now.

From Soutine, Utrillo, Modigliani and the many others who shared improvised potluck dinners washed down with cheap wine in their dimly lit, cold and drafty cells in La Ruche, their works which would casually be leaned against a dirty wall to finish drying allowing for the easel to once again be put into use all ended up in giant glass and steel buildings. These once wild animals now tamed so that well fed upper middle-class tourists can give a quick perusal between shopping trips.

It depressed me. There was also the feeling that many of the artists, were they to magically appear from the past as they had been when creating their great works, would be turned away at the door by security.

I could not imagine my life without museums but to continue to go was another type of heartache. Besides this, more and more I had begun to truly think of myself as a painter and my continued presence amongst these crowds would feel a sort of betrayal. Perusing the climate controlled galleries while outside in front of the building Soutine in a stained threadbare coat too warm for the day begs for change while standing next to the violinist and man with a drawing board on his knees doing caricatures.

By complete happenstance, as I was contemplating this resolve, the Musée de l' Orangerie was reopening after renovations. I had some friends in from out of town who really wanted to see it. Wednesday morning, between their jet lag and the fact that I am an inherently early riser, we got there right as it was opening and with no one else around.

Seeing the Soutine(s) that I had read about; being able to sit alone on the black backless divan and commune with them, renewed my faith in museums but with specific conditions.

One important thing to do is get to the museum early, just as they are opening their doors. Of course, after the initial early opening hours there is no avoiding the crowds. The ability to spend an indefinite amount of time in front of a work, quietly contemplating it is not realistic.

If you cannot get to one of the bigger museums when it firsts opens, do not bother. The crowds and noise encountered any time after noon negate having a real experience with the work.

People start at the top of a museum, working their way down. On a subconscious level at least, this is often about feeling that they got their money's worth. It is easy to become desensitized or even indifferent to beauty. This is the surest way to do it. It is almost as if the mind goes into protective mode obscuring the sensations of all that you are seeing, lest it overwhelm. To go top to bottom is the equivalent of eating an entire plate of cake frosting flowers. It will at best reduce down the experience to retaining the names of the works seen but not the sensations nor impressions.

In this digital age, it is easy to read up beforehand about what is in a museum's collection(s). Pick a few pieces that interest you, head in that general direction while stopping to look at things in the salons around it.

Using this method, potentially entire floors could be skipped but what is seen will stay with you is more than mere lists of names alone.

Of course, in playing devil's advocate, one could question the potential loss of discovering a work or painter of whom there had been no previous knowledge. There is that possibility but realistically there is a greater chance for the mere casual art fan and museum goer to benefit more from this method than the risk of losing discovery.

Another argument against my methodology is that not everyone will find themselves back in Europe once a year. Their time at the Louvre or Centre Pompidou may very well be their only go at it.

Less is still more. Better to look at a handful of works and really retain memory of them than an entire building's worth which becomes a fatigue inducing sort of visual babel.

Time, to a certain extent is the skin which history not so much wears as is covered by, becoming thicker with every passing year.

Politicians, artists, soldiers and philosophers become two dimensional, pressed down on either side by their birth and death dates.

Even when one of the better biographers tried to reinsert humanity via interesting anecdotes, there remains that once removed effect of the subject trapped or merely preserved under museum glass.

Regardless of how often we have read of Mozart's love for billiards or the excited huffing of Zola sitting down to table, one cannot imagine encountering them attached to the mundane aspects of existence, such as thirsty, with bad breath, walking slower until a pair of new shoes are broken in.

The humanity, even when written about remains a sort of abstraction in the same way that occurs when visiting someone in hospital. There is awareness of what the words describing their predicament mean, however devoid of experiencing sensations one's self, it's an intellectual exercise in familiar abstractions.

This detachment that accompanies that which we know but do not experience directly can happen when reading a compelling biography.

In the detached state, it is easy to imagine how we would handle a situation. We are not starving, he, they were. So it is easy enough to say to one's self;

"I would have.."

I had been reading the life of some twentieth century author. It was not very good. At one point after establishing his reputation he became blocked. The emotion of such a thing most likely effected his decision making process. Instead of shaking things up to see what happened, he stayed rigidly to his established schedule and methodology, remaining blocked.

It got me to thinking of my own creative process with my visual works. I want a style but to never lapse into mere mannerisms.

I would remain disciplined in regard to my work ethic but would also avoid an over ritualization of the process as to prevent potentially ever trapping myself.

I was not now forsaking them but I would have one season of not going to any museums. Initially I was at peace with my decision. But as my time in Paris loomed up, I had some trepidations. What if I was making a mistake? I would then have a year of regretting it. This thought though steeled my resolve. A year of regret was a finite amount of time. I knew that I would be back.

Realistically, even were my plan ill advised, my mind would surely wander to many other things, it was a near on impossibility that regret would remorselessly hammer away at me for an entire year.

One thing which made it seem almost as if I were negating my resolution was how compelling the city remains aesthetically outside of the museums and galleries.

Aside from all the interesting public sculptures, the city is a work of art unto itself. It is a masterpiece spreading out over centuries and mediums. The buildings, the odd little details to be found on the wrought iron grate work of doors and balcony railings.

Paris is called the city of light and rightfully so. It is a misconception though to immediately think of the Champ Elysees or some such other similar luminescent spot.

It is the ambient light. The little side streets which I hold a deep affection for, seemingly not modernized any more than from the time of Flaubert.

There is to be found, a delicate yellow, small areas of the left bank as viewed through a thin slice of amber smuggled over in 1917 by a fleeing white Russian. Or sometimes a faint green, my daily Pernod given too much water after Louise insisted upon serving me.

I have tried to capture these distinctive glows with camera as to show friends but it never works out. Akin to snapping a photo of some mythic creature only to find it has jumped out of frame as finger depresses button. My friends were never sure what they were supposed to be looking at and so I have finally given up; keeping these mellow golds and faint emeralds for myself.

The sky too has its own distinct cadence of light. At night, correspondence and chapter of the book kept by the side of the bed finished, I lay on my side looking at the top of the Val de Grace. If it is lightly raining or had been, then the sky is an odd sort of flat silver, a vintage movie screen or antique mirror meant more for show than practical use.

Other times, the sky is a dark blue which seems to pulse between that and a darkish near on purple that is in sympathy with its stygian hues. It is the color of mussels or something else which has spent its life in the depths out of sight from man.

As a young boy, I remember when it was first expected of me that I was to firmly shake hands upon meeting someone. I was pleased, since I knew that I had a firm grip and it seemed this was the first step, entrée into the real world, the world of adults. Of course, in America men still shake hands but there is nothing behind it now. It is the last vestige of a forgotten ritual, divorced from any connection of association with giving one's word or other matters of etiquette and honor.

People in America still say: "I promise" or even less formal vows and they mean it so long as it is convenient to them or they do not forget.

There has been trouble in and around France. It is, stateside an immediate cause célèbre. From the comfort of their homes overseas people weigh in with sympathetic phrases.

I do not say anything publicly but to those who ask of my usual residency, I say that I stand as I always have, with France and with my friends. It sounds good and noble too. I mean it though.

Partially, I do not have a choice. Were I to live there full time, as is my ultimate ambition, then I would not be able to just pack up and leave whenever anything bad were to occur.

No one says anymore about it to me after my initial pronouncement.

Back in the city, my city, the usual time. There are visibly less tourists which I do not mind.

Everyone is surprised and moved to see me. There is no way that I could stay away. I do believe though that there is such a thing as tempting fate.

For only the second time but for different reasons than the first, I decide to forgo museums. It is not fear based but this time I do not have the slightest reservation about going without.

Putting aside the superficial "flash a peace sign" as their photo is snapped in front of a Van Gough crowd, why do we go to museums?

Paintings have now become even more a commodity, blue chips painters etc. They are now equally if not more a dollar signs as much as any kind of spiritual or intellectual touchstone.

So many great works are now far down the corridor of time from their initial conception that we cannot view them as any kind of barometer for the zeitgeist. Nor are they any longer able to serve as heralds for a new era. To view them mainly in historical context is to also miss the point.

Why do we go to museums as the average citizen will never own any of these works or even things similar?

We go, and it is not merely a being an artist thing, to add to ourselves in one of the abstract equations which constitute an "I".

We go to find new ways to contemplate that which we already know or add another layer to the inner soliloquy.

This year, I was not thinking in terms of substitution, it just naturally happened which is the best way for anything to occur. I received the same intellectual/spiritual payoff walking the Jardin de Plantes, looking out my window at all hours of the day to see the different faces that the buildings wore depending upon the hour as I would have at a museum.

4:30 AM. Momentarily I stir. The tinny sound of a scooter, finally going home, echoes off of the still sleeping buildings. It is Romeo, he is tired but does not mind for he believes that his life will turn out exactly the way he imagines it.

I turn over. What will I do the tomorrow that is now an early today?

It does not matter as I am truly here, I will return.

Totem Thoughts: Mendelsohn & Goethe

"You go, I am going to stay and sit at the end of the bar faking wisdom" I said to her. She knew that it was my way of telling her that I was now working without sounding pretentious. If nothing else, we had learned how to avoid conflict arising from me being distracted by having one foot in that *other place* where the words danced while waiting to be sculpted when we were out and about. She was gracious and I offered to make her dinner tomorrow night which was nice of me but not without agenda as it was a subtle way of telling her that she should sleep at her own place tonight. She said "OK." keeping her voice devoid of all tension and disappointment. She kissed me good night, these kisses were always among her best for at the very least, on a subconscious level she resolved to put extra effort into them as to show me what I was missing out on. I watched her walk away trying to guess if she would take a taxi or head to the train. Before I got my answer, a truck appeared and by the time it slowly crawled away she was gone. I had one more solitary drink as I felt the ink just below my skin begin to percolate. Briefly I felt the ache of what I had denied myself but then the words churned within me. I nodded at the waitress as I got up. She winked at me and from what I had observed in the past was thinking too of Cecilia as her lips took on the slight smile.

I had walked home to burn off a little of the excess energy and better focus. Settling down to business I pulled the cap off of my pen. The nib section remained stuck inside with the ink cartridge section attached to that trailing behind it. I looked at the empty barrel in my left hand and got a queasy feeling, it was akin to the odd embarrassment of seeing a good friend seriously hurt.

My mind flashed back to the hunting trip with Sidney, a lone drunken hunter across the stream startled awake by our approach, the buckshot stuck in his shoulder which I had to pick out, first with the tip of my pen knife, then for the bigger pieces, my fingers. He mostly avoided me after that even though he emphatically agreed with everyone that he was lucky that I had been there as I was one of his cooler headed friends but on those social occasions with invitations which we both had to accept he always upon encountering me averted his gaze from mine. I was quickly able to re-attach the barrel with several twists but with the first few words I put down I momentarily shuddered. It was passing though, I shook it off and it was just me again and blank white paper waiting to be ravaged.

The first word was the strongest, powerful in its purity. It linked its arms through the one that followed and so on, each now pulling the proceeding one after it like participants of a May Day dance. I kept on for hours until I felt my concentration wane. I turned the lights out, left the record player on but lowered the volume and went to splash some water on my face before turning in.

I kept the light off as it would take too long to warm up anyways, giving the warm staccato buzz of a fly repeatedly hitting up against a window pane as it demands its freedom. There was enough ambient light spilling in from the street as I had only half closed the door. The sink was sunken into the counter. In this light, with its shape: a giant ghostly white ear, only instead of whispering into it I turn on the tap.

We met up the next day in the late afternoon. The clouds had been threatening violence all day but I still had held off on getting groceries as it was one of our things and I did not want to unintentionally inject any subtext into tonight's agenda. The weather was bad, the heavy curtain of rain which beat against the windows of the bar making it seem by the second round, claustrophobic. We could not go home and make dinner as originally planned for me searing up some steaks but being unable to open the windows would allow the smoke to linger and by bedtime turn the air into a heavy dead thing.

There was a movie theater with a small organic bakery on one side and on the other an even smaller gallery that specialized in African art, where Aimé Césaire once read some of his poetry. The theater offered second run movies and revivals but never anything which could remotely be mistaken for a classic. We stood under the awning looking at the small tacked up poster. With my faulty math, I estimated to have been in my late teens when the movie had originally come out.

"Do you want to go in or we could go to another bar."

She reminded me that the next bar would be no different than the last. I got us the tickets. I do not think that I had seen the movie when it had originally come out but vaguely recalled the title. Because the house lights were already out almost everybody here could chalk up their presence due to the rain as evidenced by the slow flapping of limbs towards the floor to shake the water off, worn spring red upholstered seats now temporary nests for these flightless birds.

The movie had shots and mannerisms which were initially a sort of new visual shorthand but in as little time as a year afterwards became cliché. I found myself mentally redoing the math, how old had I been? Even if I got the age wrong, I started thinking back to what I had been doing at that age, the recollection of ambitions. From that my mind further wandered, now it had nothing to do with me, I was writing about some other nineteen-year-old.

She had looked over at me, trying not to smile. By the time the movie ended, the rain had stopped. We could now go grab some groceries and make dinner but I wanted to take a detour to Olivier's for a drink.

We sat, I still had one foot in that other place, lost in thought, filling up more pages in my head. Even without a pen in my hand, she could always tell when I was working. She teased; telling me that she could not believe a crappy movie like that had inspired anything.

"It was not the actual movie but the time frame that got me thinking, dancing with secret ghosts.

We both ate too much, too fast. For me, on a subconscious level I think I had been spurred on by revisiting in my head those lean years, it was an affirmation that I had made it out and could have as much of anything as I wanted. For her, she desired to keep up with me, matching me stroke for stoke as to reiterate in all our appetites we were still evenly matched. I was able to open the windows but the air was wet and heavy, the sky had been crying and would not take any scent nor heat into her as to keep her sorrow pure. It was a fitful sleep we fell into after doing filthy things to each other on full stomachs. In the middle of the night, she pressed herself against the wall, not to avoid intimacy but because she was burning hot and the smooth plaster of it offered some coolness.

More and more the new piece was gestating within me soon to be birthed out. We had coffee together at the café by the subway station before she headed off to work. There was a pervading peace and I just hoped that when I messed it up it was done in an imaginative way.

I went home and started writing. Around lunchtime I went out to grab a bite to eat and people watch. I wandered down the Rue de la Huchette just to give myself an excuse to go into the Tunisian bakery whose masterpieces were always on display in the window, piled high one atop another and brazenly sexual in both shape and glistening stickiness. I came out with two white paper bags that still managed to give off a cloying perfume of honey and rosewater despite being twisted shut. Everyone should aspire to constantly be evolving. Most people do not, confusing evolution with change which is more passive as change happens but usually due to an outside force and not any kind of natural rhythm. The resolution to change is somewhat to miss the point as change is how we are after a thing regardless of whether we were the progenitor of it or not where as evolution's progress cannot be controlled but the phenomena itself can be fostered via a hungry intellect, fed all the things that we should be pulling towards ourselves.

I saw a girl who looked like Magda but as she had looked back then. She was another lifetime ago. Even had it been her I saw no point in talking to her now. The me that she knew was long dead. I would not say something faux noble such as;

"I have changed" as we can only live through our own history. She would find the current me a bastard too as I had traded in destructiveness for a singular focus on my work which everything in my life must now be in service of.

Scenes that I have not thought of in years come flooding back. My head tings like an empty coffee can in which a rapid non-stop stream of pennies is thrown into. I had the compulsion not to see her again but merely gaze up close at her doppelganger as to see what other half-forgotten histories came back. There was the small tear in my left knee from where I went down, the pantomiming of tying my shoe as I waited for her to emerge from the café, bill paid. The cashier was chatting her up. I did not blame him but grew annoyed all the same. Clearly, she did not have all day to linger or she would not have opted to stand by the bar to have her coffee.

The precious gem of a perfect past summer was smashed up. A shimmering dust, devalued as it settles and mixes with the pavement making it sparkle when the light hits It just right but despite its pedigree, ultimately being worth nothing. Through the cloth of my pants, my knee continued to feel the rough bite of the gravel. I straightened up. Ah baby I had seen enough. My thoughts traveled all over the place. I poked around my record store to center myself but the small paper cups of strong coffee always offered up to me and the place's inherent heat did not do much to even me out. I sit in the bird park across the street transferring my purchases into my book bag. I am relaxing again. Not that she would have cared to but were she to become a fly on the wall, being told right beforehand that "I had won" she would not be shown a flashy car nor beautiful wife with whom the satisfaction of her body aside I had little in common with. All she would see is me with my ability if I so desired to spend the entire day laying on the couch reading, which was all I had ever really wanted, to sit and think deep thoughts, sort of a modern day Thoreau with a stack of Jelly Roll Morton records.

I had recently reread Henry David Thoreau (1817-1862). I liked his emphasis on the importance of an inner life and his largely impractical in the modern world ideas on a sort of naturalist humanism, all couched in a poetical narrative. In the past, a turn off for me was what had soured some of his direct contemporaries (Robert Louis Stevenson considered it all "self-indulgent sulking" and Nathaniel Hawthorne "A modern savage, taking himself away from all society"). Although not working within the framework of any group, movement or institution, it somewhat smacked of a sort of self-indulgent academicism; someone spending years writing their dissertation on how many times *pears* appear in Chaucer.

Although completely unintentional, I often gravitated towards writers who were a mix of thinker and men of action. Men such as Stendhal (1783-1842 part of Napoleon's invading army of Russia 1812), Isaak Babel (1894-1940 army commander of the 1st cavalry, which was considered the toughest) and many others, bookshelves full. They need not have gone to war to have been men of action; it is a matter of being out in the world experiencing things first hand without utilizing the insulation of title or money. Very rarely did an artist born of privilege go out into the world to enmesh themselves in everyday society. That is not to say they did not travel but that it was just without any of the privation of war, poverty etc. which colored and added to the chops of their more boots on the ground peers.

Talking in an inaccurate shorthand, Johann Wolfgang von Goethe (1749-1832) is sometimes portrayed to have just arrived in Weimar, Germany where through some kind of Faustian bargain he was able to sort of help rule as he pontificated on all subjects from botany to color theory to the human Skeleton. Although there would be a few moments of discord with his father when he initially wanted to give up his career as jurisprudence for writing and some soured affairs of the heart, he more often than not had smooth sailing but was actually an exception to the rule of the privileged artist.

He was born into a good and supportive family, showing a precocious intellect, initially training to be a lawyer. Always intellectually hungry his father fostered Goethe's pursuits with lessons so that by an early age he was multi lingual, a lover of classical literature and an accomplished artist. Although he wanted to become a lawyer, with his progressive humanist philosophy he did not enjoy practicing law. An attempt at making a living as editor would prove so financially impractical he would return to practicing again.

Throughout his early life he had always been writing. During his last go at being a lawyer (1772) he had written *The Sorrows of Young Werther* (1774) which won him wide spread fame. With its amped up emotions, over (cold) logical reason it, along with the nascent *Sturm Und Drang movement* can be said to be one of the early building blocks of the Romantic Era (1800-1870-ish). It was upon the strength and popularity of this novel that Carl August the Duke of Saxe-Weimar-Eissenach invited him to Weimar (1775).

Goethe would still travel most notably to Italy for two years but for the rest of his life Weimar would be his home. He possessed both genius and talent with the added advantage that he knew how to deftly navigate the corridors of power. His life in Weimar was not merely the existence of a well-cared for court pet. After only a year in Weimar he was granted citizenship and appointed to the Geheimer Legationstrat being given a seat along with its accompanying vote, one of the states' highest offices.

From the start of their earliest meeting, Goethe was a close friend and confidant to the Duke which made it easy for his intelligence to be gauged and utilized. While being a great thinker he was not a mere passive observer. He was ennobled in 1782, the titled "von" being added to his name. Along with the Duke he would participate in the battle of Valmy against revolutionary France and in the siege of Mainz (1792). Over the course of the next five decades he would help actively guide Weimar's destiny culturally, politically and intellectually. He would hold a variety of important posts which were hands on not merely honorific in title. From being appointed head of Commission for War and Roads construction to scientific inquiries into such wide-ranging fields which included theory of colors, metamorphosis of plants, human anatomy where he discovered the intermaxillary bone and meteorology where he came up with a valid theory on decreasing barometric pressure and storms utilizing glass (Goethe Barometers).

Although much more a sui generis than Goethe, I have always associated in my mind Mendelssohn with the master of Weimar. Both had vast intellect that allowed them to do many things at once and well. The difference, age aside, being that Goethe's professional pursuits were all for the reward of intellectual stimulation whereas Mendelssohn's were all in service of music. Felix Mendelssohn's (1809-1847) life, premature death aside seems to be the exception to the rule of composers and their typical accompanying tragic biography.

He was born in Hamburg (Germany) the son of Abraham, a banker whose sense of organization he would inherit. Felix's parents always emphasized the importance of intellectual pursuits via their lifestyle. This life of the mind started with his grandfather who was a famous philosopher, Moses Mendelssohn (1729-1786) to whom the moniker "The Modern Plato" was given. Moses dialogue on the immortality of the soul was translated into dozens of languages and counted among its admirers Immanuel Kant (1724-1804), Johann Gottfried Herder (1744-1803) and Mirabeau (1749-1791). His mother, Leah was also highly intelligent, specializing in linguistics, reading classical Greek literature in the original language. As a child his family moved to Berlin when Napoleon's troops were invading, taking up residence with their grandmother on the fashionable Neu Promenade where their salon quickly became one of the centers of artistic and intellectual life.

Abraham was progressive in his thinking but knew he was not as intellectual as his wife and father. He was fine with this though and built up the family fortune as it allowed him to contribute to the foundation of his family. The zeitgeist in Germany and Austria at this time was that intelligence combined with money, which was used to further feed it, could be equated to prestige whereas without the funds which allowed intellectualism to be comfortably pursued it was mere bohemianism, often a shorthand for dirt morally or physically. The dichotomy between some of his family's intellectualism and his own could have been a source of resentment, stymieing all intellectual pursuits. Instead he always bore it with grace once his son's fame and talent were confirmed constantly good naturedly saying; "First I was the son of my father, now I am the father of my son." By way of explaining where he fit in the family tree between two generations of famed intellectuals. And along similar lines; "I am but a dash uniting Moses and Felix."

For the entire family intellectual pursuits were a part of everyday life, like eating. When only three years old, Felix's mother had started teaching him and his equally talented sister Fanny piano. Abraham had to go to Paris on business bringing along the entire family and a piano teacher whom Leah had engaged for the journey. Once back in Berlin Felix and Fanny's formal music and academic education began. Felix studied piano with Ludwig Burger and theory with Karl Friedrich Zeher. While studying music he also studied violin, languages and drawing which would allow him to become an accomplished illustrator/watercolorist for the rest of his life. His parents did not pamper Felix though which prevented him from ever merely being a precocious wunderkind. He had to get up each day at dawn and put in a full day of studies but as to avoid any resentment when he got older they did incorporate time for play too.

Felix possessed a sensitive ear and fantastic memory along with musical intuition which allowed him to easily absorb lessons. By the age of nine he was talented enough for public piano recitals. A year later he joined The Singakademie which was directed by one of his teachers, Zelter. This served as his initial introduction to choral music which he would maintain a lifelong interest in. At this point he also began composing. It only took him two years before he was writing fully realized pieces in various genres, showing the concentration and discipline of an adult. In just one year (1821) his pen produced symphonies, fugues, string quartets, two operas and a handful of smaller works.

Abraham's belief that Felix had a destiny and would be considered a great man was a catalyst for the families' conversion to Christianity. His wife's family had been pushing for this move for years which he had initially stubbornly refused. But anti-Semitism would have affected the trajectory of Felix's career and severely limited his options. The lynchpin moment arrived when Felix came home from The Akademie crying. He had been singing in a chorus for Bach's St. Matthew's Passion when an anti-Semitic remark was made and even his teacher chuckled a little. "Bartholdy" as was added to distinguish them from the still Jewish branch of the Mendelssohn family tree.

On Sunday afternoons Leah held her music salons which were much celebrated. Professional musicians often joined the children in formal presentation of chamber music recitals. People from all walks of life would come to listen. In 1821, Karl Maria von Weber (1786-1826) was in Berlin to supervise the premier of his opera *Der Freishutz* and took time to visit the salon. At these concerts Felix played piano and led the small orchestra. Weber was impressed by what he heard and saw, returning to the Mendelssohn household whenever his schedule allowed.

In 1821, Zelter brought Felix to Weimar to introduce him to Goethe. Felix played Beethoven scores by site and Bach fugues too. Goethe had heard Mozart as a child play and felt Mendelssohn was already a greater talent. There was a 72-year gap in age yet Goethe professed to recognize his genius (Felix was 12). They became good friends and remained so right up until Goethe's death in 1832.

In 1822 the family went on a trip but Felix was never forced into the circus like child prodigy life as Mozart had been. This prevented Felix from ever chafing under the expectations or rules as Mozart eventually would and also nipped in the bud any negative Pavlovian response to structure and authority.

In Cassel (Germany) Felix impressed everybody by playing improvisations for Ludwig Spohr (1784-1859). Like Goethe, the composer also marveled at Felix's abilities. Three years later in Paris another musical luminary Luigi Cherubini (1760-1842) would be awed when Felix spontaneously set "Kyrie" for voice and orchestra. On his fifteenth birthday, Zeher proclaimed him an independent member of the brotherhood of musicians. His innate abilities combined with all the inspirations derived from his travels and studies allowed him to quickly outgrow all that his teachers had to offer him.

The further success of Abraham's business allowed the family to move to a seven acre estate in Leipziger Strasse (1825). On this spacious estate, the adjoining garden house was converted into a theater for weekly concerts. He was widely considered good looking and brilliant but never let all the accolades go to his head, maintaining the work ethos which his parents had instilled in him. "A Midsummer Night's Dream" overture, now a western classical music staple, was written when Felix was only seventeen. The first version was for two pianos and premiered at one of the garden house-theater parties, six months later Felix would direct an orchestral version in Stettin.

Seemingly music's golden child, not every shot was a bull's eye. *Hochzeit Des Camacho* was an early opera based off of an episode from Cervantes's *Don Quixote*. Composer Gaspare Spontini (1774-1851) then the director of the Berlin Opera accepted the work but kept it from production for a year. When it was finally produced it was in one of the smaller theaters. Upon finally hearing it, Mendelssohn himself found it a third-rate work and was at peace with it only being given one performance.

There were no growing pains in regard to Mendelssohn finding his destiny and his ambitions too seemed to have been fully formed from the start. He saw as two main parts of his life's mission; 1) To restore the music of Bach which had largely become forgotten 2) To found a great conservatory. He managed to rescue Bach's music which by this point was only being enjoyed by professional musicians starting with *The Passion According to St. Matthew*. The Cantor of Leipzig who had been the one to introduce Zelter to Felix possessed many Bach manuscripts, some of which had been given to him by Felix's grandfather including the only existing copy of "the Passion…"

Zelter and Felix would go over parts of this manuscript together studying it down to the smallest detail and having members of the Singakademie sing them. From these Bach nights Felix formed a group of sixteen singers to rehearse the scores choral pieces. Eduard Devrient (1801-1877) was one of the choristers and a well-known opera singer. He would participate in exhaustingly discussing the score. He helped fuel Felix's ambition towards a live performance. Together the two of them worked to get Zelter's consent to allow a Singakademie performance. Zelter believed that the world was not ready for the piece but their enthusiasm won him over. The premier was under Mendelssohn's direction in Berlin (1829).

Despite Zelter's apprehensions, the concert was a great success and the start of a Bach revival which put Bach in the cultural position he occupies today. Having met one of his life goals at an early age Mendelssohn decided to travel which would serve the dual purpose of new inspiration and contemplation of his next step. Mendelssohn visited ten countries, starting with England where he was such a hit that he premiered his "Symphony in C Minor".

He traveled onto Scotland whose landscapes would inspire "Fingal's Cave Overture" Which was actually a tone poem/programmatic music and his Symphony no 3 "Scotch" which conjured up the land and the days of Queen Mary of Scots. Throughout "The Scotch" symphony Mendelssohn incorporates rhythms and cadence suggestive of the land but it is never meant to mirror nor authentically incorporate folk forms. It is all beautiful melancholy punctuated with moments of joyous dances and a march before once again submerging into the picturesque mists. There had been to varying degrees programmatic music before Mendelssohn and it would after him sometimes become even more literal but with his well-traveled life and deep appreciation of literature he could be seen as an immediate forerunner for genres (tone poem/programmatic Music) that some of his peers would carry on with, these early efforts though helping to birth the romantic era in music.

From the UK part of his tour Mendelssohn would go onto Italy. The Italian art would inspire him to write his "Italian Symphony". Italy resonated with him too in the way the art was largely rooted in a sort of traditionalism, each generation of artist seeming to be connected to the previous with very little desire to break freely away. It was also here that Mendelssohn became more consciously aware of a sort of musical conservatism within himself. Looking at how he would help others and how some of his work stretched the boundaries of tradition his conservatism is sometimes misunderstood. He clearly, through his actions on the behalf of others showed that he did not have an either or philosophy in art but wanted the new to be built off of the old and not make radical breaks rejecting tradition outright. He was not against innovation but was deeply suspicious of anything too radical which could merely be the gimmicked and novel. From Italy, he went onto Paris where he met Chopin (1810-1849), Liszt (1811-1886) and Meyerbeyer (1791-1864). It was the early days of what so far was a very informal movement and everybody got along even in private feeling no need to get the daggers out.

Wrapping up his tour he returned to London where he premiered *Fingal 's Cave* and performed the piano part of "The Concerto in G Minor". He would return to Germany and in 1837 be appointed musical director in Dusseldorf in charge of opera, church music, and two choral bodies. This was his first go at filling an official post and from the get-go he was not happy. A major source of tension from the start was the musicians used to a lighter touch not appreciating how exacting Mendelssohn was. He expected a high level of performance from all and typically ordered more rehearsals than they were used to along with more challenging programs.

After only six months he quit but within a year found himself offered the post of musical director for the prestigious Gewandhaus Orchestra in Leipzig. Referred to as "The Pride of Leipzig", Gewandhaus and its connected concerts were subsidized by the cities linen merchants and held in the ancient market hall. The organization had a history which went back to the first half of the 18th century and Mendelssohn's embrace of artistic tradition made him the perfect artist for them. He took the post (1835) and immediately it was a good fit between artist and institution each adding further luster to the other. This year also marked the death of his father. It saddened him but he got through it by working, one of the pieces being an oratorio based on St. Paul which premiered at The Rhine Festival a mere year later.

On his way back from the festival Mendelssohn stopped in Frankfurt to visit a family named Jeanrenaud. He made repeated visits and gossip soon had it that it was for the widow who also assumed as much. In reality, it was for her seventeen-year-old daughter Cecile. Even though she had caught his eye he was still focused on his muse. He kept away from her to test himself and was surprised by how acutely he felt her absence, it was the first time he had romantically fallen for anyone.

In 1837 they married. It was a happy and peaceful union. He and his wife enjoyed each other and he was very much absorbed by and into his

Gewandhaus duties. At this time Mendelssohn began associating with Robert Schumann (1810-1856) and his future wife Clara Wieck (1819-1896). Like himself the couple had an overall serious mien and the trio's friendship was free and easy. Robert Schumann described Mendelssohn as "The Mozart of the 19th century" and for Mendelssohn's part with his friend's talent and intellectual views there was never a compromise which need be made for the sake of friendship as was the case with some of his other composer friends. He worked hard but in its overall perfection it was a rather idyllic life which was broken up in 1840 when The King of Prussia appointed him the head of a projected academy of arts in Berlin. Mendelssohn did not want to leave Leipzig but had enough savvy to know not to even consider refusing the king. Beethoven had been the first composer to break the practice of a composer affiliated with a royal court of great house being merely on par with the footman and cooks but to some extent genius was still a commodity to be bought, traded and susceptible to royal whims and political intrigues/climes. More and more composers sometimes at the risk of poverty or (social) exile would build off of the small beachhead of freedom established by Beethoven.

Mendelssohn assumed his post in 1841. There was a complex web of intrigue, with the actual academy still physically only in blueprint form. From the baroque era on in Germany and Austria music has always been intertwined with court politics. Part of the reason is the inherent propaganda to be had; one political faction backing a composer could garner support of the people through successful premiers and performances of a work for which they had been the facilitator. Culturally the opera and symphony were always attended so one was sure to be able to at least briefly corner the minister who had been evasive during office hours. Regardless of who reigned in any given area, every court and cabinet had its artist whom it backed hopefully to the detriment of those of the opposition.

A year of waiting around and in-house arguments and Mendelssohn was able to take temporary leave of Berlin for the world premiere of his Scottish Symphony (Leipzig, 1842) followed by two command performances in Buckingham palace for Queen Victoria.

Upon returning to Berlin Mendelssohn found that the plans for an academy had been abandoned. He happily offered his resignation but as to not offend the king had to take the honorary position of Kapellmeister to the king which entailed writing music for special occasion but with the benefit that he need not reside in Berlin to fulfill his duties.

While serving in this post he wrote *A Midsummer Night's Dream* suite the overture of which he had written as a teen. He also wrote music for plays. Back in Leipzig he renewed his association with the Gewandhaus, once again building up momentum for both the institution and his own reputation. Once he felt it was strong enough he made an appeal to the King of Saxony to create a conservatory (1843). The king agreed and immediately provided the funds. Having spent so much time dreaming of creating a conservatory and also absorbing what he could from the abandoned academy project the whole conservatory was pretty fast formed. Mendelssohn brought Robert Schumann aboard to help shape the piano classes. The conservatory opened under Mendelssohn's directorship in 1843.

He was now working non-stop teaching, supervising at the conservatory, conducting for Gewanhaus Orchestra, writing (oratorio "Elijah", concerto for violin and orchestra) and putting in guest appearances as conductor and occasionally pianist throughout Europe. All this activity began to affect his health and he started to experience pain in his head with excessive bouts of fatigue.

By 1846 he was in outright ill health but still went to England to conduct the premier of "Elijah" for which he received the greatest ovations of his life. Upon finally returning home he was more worn out than before yet maintained a frantic schedule for a full year. Without having taken a break Mendelssohn was asked to give a command performance of "Elijah" for Queen Victoria at the palace (1847). This year would find not just his body but also his will weakened by the death of his sister and best friend Fanny. Upon hearing of her passing he fell and ruptured a blood vessel in his head. He recovered but those close to him found him a changed man. He now often had violent depressions and fits of anger accompanied by various pains often followed by complete lack of energy. After a series of strokes similar to what had killed his grandfather and sister, Mendelssohn lay unconscious in a coma for a full day before he died. The day of his funeral there was mourning throughout most of the major European capitals. Robert Schumann served as one of the pallbearers at the funeral.

With the passage of time Mendelssohn, the man and his music have become misconstrued. Mendelssohn can be seen to be one of the first romanticists, although never fully taking the leap stylistically, or as the last classicist. The romantic components of his work are clearly visible in how his pieces often combined passion and a programmatic approach which would regularly be mined by his more outright romantic leaning peers. The classicist in him utilized an adherence to rigid traditional structures of classical and baroque era counterpoint. He was actually a musical conservative being open minded to innovations as they could occur within an already established framework. This conservatism is not to be seen as reason to avoid his work. His ethos was to build off of tradition while not being limited nor trapped by it. Although taken up by almost all of his musical (romantic) peers for his revolutionary artistic proclivities, Beethoven for his part in some ways could be seen to be in the same philosophical camp as Mendelssohn having found in his day most of his symphonic hero Mozart's (1756-1791) operatic oeuvre immoral and so un-enjoyable.

I enjoy Mendelssohn's works but definitely lean towards his chamber pieces and smaller works as opposed to his symphonies (excepting his Scottish and one or two others). My reason is that they are often pretty or beautiful but without too many shifts of emotional gears or terribly varied colorations. I have the same issue with Haydn's symphonies (1732-1809). Both artists were important contributors to the Western Classical tradition but I prefer more layered complexity regardless of a composer's era. Within Mendelssohn's symphonic work there is a grace which is so naturally occurring that it would be easy and a mistake to chalk it up to a lack of substance, being only aural lightness. As much as Mendelssohn's symphonic work does not appeal to me for a certain lack of tension derived from moments of discordance as can be found to varying degrees in works by Brahms, Mahler, Berlioz and Schumann it should not be considered flaccid. Conversely, the Violin concerts by virtuoso Violinist/composer Nicolo Paganini (1782-1840) teem with drama yet were one to remove the actual soloist parts from the pieces they would very much be found to be lacking and structurally dull. Among the nicer insults Wagner issued about Mendelssohn's work was that it was too cerebral and lacked passion but beauty need not always possess, a notion that in one way or another was counter to the basic tenants of the romantics.

Mendelssohn now too is painted as someone who was always happy go lucky, one hand jotting down the latest works as the other waved goodbye or hello to one of his many friends. He did not have it easy in regard to things just being handed to him. The effortless parts were the innate   support lent him by his parents and the facility with which he would later conduct himself in the charged politics of his field. Both of these factors were combined with the fact that he had such a clear-cut vision of the destiny he wanted to pursue even from his career's nascence. He could be with orchestras under his baton demanding and exacting in what he expected. Always for Mendelssohn the vision of what he wanted and how to do it was easy but he still worked for it in a disciplined way adopted since early childhood.

Another "easy" aspect of his personality which has since been used to gloss over the man as a whole were his dealings with his peers. Shortly after his death *the war of the romantics* which saw a lot of the preeminent composers taking sides in what boiled down to a school of traditionalism based out of Leipzig and represented by then widowed Clara Schumann and Johann Brahms versus Franz Liszt and Richard Wagner's "Music of the Future" coming out of Weimar. The discord arriving from differing aesthetical values and opinions did not arise over night or after Mendelssohn died, the opposing views and their accompanying feelings had always been there yet in his lifetime he repeatedly offered a helping hand and use of his power to what would later become an enemy camp.

Liszt had dubbed Mendelssohn and his camp "The Little Leipzigers" feeling that they were holding back the progress of 19th century music. In his conservatism Mendelssohn was not a fan of Liszt's virtuosic fantasies which he felt were highly gimmicked and important only as a flashy evening's out novelty. Liszt's first virtuoso tour brought him first to the highly progressive Prague which ate up everything he had to offer then onto Leipzig which had by this time had once again deeply embraced Bach, a former resident. Before the concert started there was already a negative air as Liszt had the traditional practice of the cities important people receiving free tickets suspended. The concert was full of the fiery showmanship Liszt had been utilizing all tour but which did not win the musically conservative audience over. Liszt took sick to his bed for several days. Mendelssohn noted that to him a lot of it sounded like "Tom foolery and musical pranks" Despite his opinion of the concert, both Schumann and Mendelssohn visited Liszt during his convalescence. In his diaries and letters to others Liszt praises Mendelssohn's "extraordinarily cultured and versatile mind" and Schumann's over all absorption with music.

Mendelssohn arranged for a concert at Gewandhaus which he personally rented out. It was for musical professionals and fans. He engaged the services of 250 singers and players and had mulled wine and cakes served.

Mendelssohn purposely chose music for the program which were not known to Liszt so that he could not showboat and which were also more in line with the public's palette. Bach's "Concerto in D-Minor for 3 Pianos" was played by Liszt, Mendelssohn and Ferdinand Hiller (1811-1885) along with Schubert's "Symphony in C Major" which was still in manuscript form. This concert done in a more serious and (perceived) respectful vein managed to win Leipzig over. Another concert two days later found Liszt being royally received by the audience. Liszt declared that he would do a benefit concert for a cause of the locals' choice. He had to travel to Dresden for a previously committed benefit concert then back to Leipzig. With its four hour journey time and to us, primitive travel conditions, it is even more impressive that Liszt made up the Leipzig benefit program spontaneously and included works by Mendelssohn, Schumann and Hiller with the proceeds going to benefit a musicians' retirement home. This concert too was a success. Some of what he had witnessed institutionally would give Liszt ideas for what he would institutionally create in Weimar.

Once he was free and clear of Leipzig with his reputation intact his appreciation seemed to wane somewhat. In the initial years of his artistic prominence which largely started with this first tour as he conceptualized new forms he showed little desire to compromise with what would become "the other side". Even in his letters to others more directly in his circles, he after the fact gives Mendelssohn and Schumann their props but more for their traits that were already known and apparent to others while the rest of his praise is a sort of verbal boomerang of congratulating them on being wise enough to admire him. In his diaries and correspondence Mendelssohn occasionally would comment in the negative but he did not openly and actively feud even helping some of his peers who had a drastically different artistic mission. It can be chalked up to class but also a sort of economy of energy not wanting to waste any of futile feuds of semantics and theory. It should not be forgotten that while he was being helpful and nice he had little patience for what he perceived as ignorance or ineptness especially with his musicians and was never shy of letting them know his displeasure, sometimes explosively.

A more lasting positive example of his good nature was the friendship between Berlioz and himself. Mendelssohn had initially met Berlioz in Italy where they spent much time together. As radical as Berlioz's works were sometimes considered by the public and critics both he and Mendelssohn shared a deep love of antiquity, utilizing aspects of the past as inspiration for their works. Their association began well before the war of the romantics and was never touched by it. Within their own work the men had little in common even though on a technical level in Berlioz's music there could have been found parts of the working theories partially in line with not just the Leipzigers but a little from both sides, a radical traditionalism. Later on, this artistic midway along with his French nationality and preoccupation chasing his own muse would for the most part keep Berlioz free of the fray. One area with no shades of gray where the two artists could easily meet was that both men were deeply moved by art outside of their medium, especially literature.

In 1843 Berlioz visited Germany for the first time. He met Schumann who had invited him some six years earlier. He rekindled his acquaintance with Mendelssohn too. By this time Mendelssohn was comfortably handling all the politics of the musical world. Berlioz was a composer of equal intelligence but was destined career wise to never have nearly as easy of a go of it as his friend. Graciously Mendelssohn facilitated two concerts for Berlioz in Leipzig at Gewandhaus. It was a great leg up for Berlioz and a moral shot in the arm. This underlined both Mendelssohn's overall class and also the deep level of their friendship. Mendelssohn liked Berlioz the man but was, a few of his melodies aside, never a fan of his work. Berlioz was well aware of this yet the two composers would publicly praise each other's work time and again. Even after Mendelssohn's death, Berlioz would hold his work in the highest esteem his whole life. Berlioz was stoic about his good friend's lack of enjoyment from his work;

"We are both in search of beauty but going down different paths."

Before heading back to France, Berlioz and Mendelssohn exchanged conducting batons as a sign of friendship and solidarity. Both men having read and been fans of James Fenimore Cooper's (1789-1851) *The Last of The Mohicans* the event would be referenced by Berlioz in correspondence as the time they exchanged tomahawks. Mendelssohn was classy but not naïve or overly non-stop cheerful. He often wrote beautiful things but they were never vapid. There is more to be found in the man and his work than what the shorthand of history has made him.

We all make totems of the art we enjoy and also our tragedies. It is a way to connect ourselves to them and also explain something about it to ourselves, the worth or effect. Mendelssohn like Schubert died young but left behind a large body of work. It is easy now through the lens of time to nod to ourselves and say, "It is as if they knew the clock was ticking." But I know from personal experience that more likely it was just that they enjoyed working and being artists that was what they did. It is also tempting to play the intellectual "what if" game. Had he lived another decade, dozen years, quarter century, how would the man and his art have changed? Maybe not at all except in small ways, new authors discovered to write a piece off of, tours further afield as European politics changed and new courts beckoned. I think of myself, I am constantly exploring, new music, authors, painters but largely my ambitions have not terribly changed.

To be able to spend all day at desk or on the couch book in hand…

I got some good pages down, in my head the story was written I just needed now to physically put it all on paper and that is always the easy part. I invite her over for dinner. At first there is a slight worry in her voice;

"Did you already go to the market?"

Everything was all right again when I told her no, that I was waiting for her and would meet her there. I grabbed my yellow mesh bag and headed out the door.

We drizzled a little olive oil on the squid and threw it in the skillet until the underside of each arm matched the color of the Fuchsias that seemed to hang from every balcony.

"Tonight we will dance?" She asked reaching for the wine. I said "maybe" but we both knew that I meant no and that it did not really matter.

IN SERVICE OF BEAUTY: D'INDY & THE SCHOLA CANTORUM

Being an author, unlike a musician or even a painter with the opening night of a show; one never gets the satisfaction via immediate feedback from an audience once a piece is done. With luck, there are some mentions and positive reviews spaced out but those too are to be read alone over morning coffee as the birds stir in the window box, shaking the dew from the geraniums so that even these small triumphs are entwined with desolation.

Rebecca commented on the fact that I was always working but I could not tell what the deeper implications were as a sea of emotion was roaring in my ears, obscuring what may have been important subtext. Instinctually I knew the clock of "us" was ticking down. We were now entering into the phase where everything was a last. The last time we would eat at a certain brasserie together, the last time we would walk the Jardin, with her tentatively reaching for my hand as I told her of Buffon. Part of me felt that despite the neglectful aspect of it, she would have been more understanding if "I am working" said to her on a Friday night had been more of shorthand for doing something without her or that I ought not to, rather than the actual at desk with pen truth. I beat down the compulsion to discuss it with her as even if we found a way through this it would just be something else anyways and at least with this I was in the right, her losing points every time I said I would be at home working and over the interim of the night I would get a hang up call checking to see if I were actually at home.

It is not by what we want that is denied us nor by desires satiated, it is by being among other people if even only temporarily that one seeks to reassert their humanity through collaborative acts such as cocktails or fucking. Every artist must retreat within themselves. This self-imposed exile is bearable but only if you can control when the fast is broken, otherwise it becomes heartache; the chaffing under circumstances not of our own making. To emerge once again regardless of the chops garnered, at first being amongst others, the sensation is as strange as you are to them but the novelty wears off and eventually comes the desire to just be alone again. This desire is a different kind of heartache but at least alone, after a while one learns a truth about oneself.

She was going to go home for a while; this country had never held the same appeal to her and now she had no reason to stay. I offered to accompany her to the train. Walking to the station had been strange, all of the familiar store fronts we had passed so often together, here we were walking by them once again yet this time was different as it was the last and we both knew it. Despite how familiar it all was, everything seemed slightly opaque as if sadness had lowered a thin gauze curtain, distorting the view of once comforting facades. Even the station, not a location tied in with our daily life, yet here too we had been more than once to begin a journey, together. Now the station was akin to an enemy whose face bore a slight resemblance to that of a friend. Nervous energy, we got there too early. I knew that I could not just say my good bye and leave her to linger alone.

The lack of any other plan I nod at the café with my chin, ignoring my own inner voice which tells me that coffee will not be good as I remind myself it is not about the coffee.

She took a seat, pushing her bag under the table with her feet. All the times we had traveled together, the hot debates the night before as I insisted that she was packing too heavy. Now here she was with merely her tiny overnight bag. I got two coffees and some pastries even though I did not desire any of it. Mechanically, without a word being said we made everything on our table disappear. The two spoons lay face up in a nest of crumbs, the plate underneath now that it held no more, all but forgotten. Two tiny versions of the ceiling fan spun on the concave surfaces of their heads creating the illusion of rapid blinking. Several times I found myself about to make one of our usual little jokes, as if this were merely a prelude to one of our trips, which would have been horrible for the both of us. Finally, it was time.

I walked her to the security turnstile. I wanted to say something profound and perhaps comforting too for if we should meet in the future most likely she would not be receptive to anything I had to say. She made a little sound in the back of her throat and I settled for merely bending down slightly hurting my neck for as in her vengeance it was a slow kiss. Her eyes took on a limpidity which under different circumstances would have been beautiful. I offered up a "I am sorry" whose lameness I compounded with an almost worse "Please, take care."

I watched her present her passport and go through the turnstile, frozen to the spot for all the good it would do me for at least five minutes after even though I had no idea what vague thought had kept me rooted there. I was distracted and could not work so wandered around not even being able to bring myself to plan what to have for dinner.

Briefly I went home and felt a lack of her presence. I told myself it was no different than the times that I had a lot of work to do and had made her take some of her stuff home because I felt the clutter was inhibiting my ability to think. I headed down Rue Soufflot peering into windows without any real desire. I was looking through a stack of postcards. A woman had a little boy in a stroller whom she was letting cough all over everybody. It would not be so bad but it was a horrible sounding cough, like a large dog being slowly strangled. She seemed oblivious to his plight, rooting around in her pocketbook for something. He was living in two worlds, before and during these painful attacks, the journey occurred always too rapidly to allow his eyes to adjust and take anything in. I shot her two looks, of annoyance and concern but both were met with indifference.

I went home and filled my day with mundane busy work: filling my pens, lighter and watering my plants. I just dropped some eggs on toast for dinner. I woke up very early the next morning which I thought a good start; only to discover that my head felt sloshy and now being vertical the drain causing a fit-series of sneezes followed by a post nasal drip nausea. I had a cold or flu. I took the first day to just rest up, taking some medicine, which put me to sleep earlier than usual. The next day upon waking up I felt better but as my morning progressed once again I felt under the weather. A nap and meal of hot comfort foods only alleviated things for several hours as did a hot bath. The only good things to come from this was that during the dips in the day when I once again became congested you could hear it in my voice and the veracity of my begging off on being taken out to drink away my blues was not questioned.

After five days, anyone I talked to sympathetically agreed that bad colds could linger. I was more than happy to agree with them as I stubbornly refused to see a doctor for no logical reason. My illness became sort of integrated into my schedule. When I first woke up I would feel fine. I experimented seeing if working or not aggravated my condition. It did not seem to make much of a difference nor did the fact that I was not smoking and eating right. Shortly after lunch regardless of how hectic my morning had been I would find that I could not keep my eyes open and would have to nap.

Three weeks into being sick and I went to the doctor. My annoyance at having spent the morning wasted in his waiting room was tempered by the good news that it was nothing serious and all I could do was what I was doing, the list of which he ran down anyways:

"Plenty of rest, eat right…."

I was working still but at a much slower pace than was my norm. I still felt the need aside from the obvious necessity of getting groceries to be out a little everyday hoping that the fresh air too would help some. I kept the circuit of my walks shorter than would have been usual had I been at one hundred percent. I was on Boulevard Saint Michel, I felt myself fatigued again and that brought on a frustration. A new plan formed in my head. I would do nothing for a day or two, work but from bed and eat foods designed to bring me back to health.

I stopped at one of the bookstores that had tables out front, browsing as I formed a list in my head of what I would need. There were some records mixed in with the coffee table books on Ingres and Rodin. Randomly I flipped through the piles. There was an album of music by D'Indy of whom I was not totally familiar but the painting on the cover with its suggestion of warmth caught my eye. I bought that along with a few postcards although I was not yet sure who I would send them to.

At the market I bought several heads of garlic, a kilo of potatoes and a small forest of leeks whose tops poked out from the horizon line of my bag. I decided that I would slightly alter my plan to get the chicken from my boucherie every day as to avoid doing too much cooking.

I slept poorly that night and I opened wide all the windows to freshen the place up before heading out to the market. I had been too out of sorts to make coffee so stopped at Martine's. She sized me up with her dark eyes, I am sure that she had heard the news but showed amazing discretion in not yet making a play. The coffee made me feel better but I knew it would not last. I told her I would see her soon, mentioning that I was fighting a cold so that she did not think my coloring was merely sadness. I had been out too early and the chickens doing laps on the rotisserie were not yet ready. I poked around the store which sold a little of everything a sort of hardware store combined with a bazar but more organized. The front of the store had large mesh baskets whose original use I did not know but were now filled with inexpensive rayon scarves in floral patterns, books of all sizes and subjects in a mish mash of languages and records. I found another D'Indy record and instinctually bought it and some slippers which would prove to be too small.

I got home and felt wiped out. I put on one of the records I bought, the first, and lay down. I instantly enjoyed the work as it employed some vaguely familiar devices but in a different way.

The next day I decided to take a walk which would not be longer only differing in route. The sun was out and the heat momentarily made me feel better. I found myself walking towards the Port Royal market. I had walked by the red and gold sign of The Schola Cantorum I do not know how many times and had never noticed that among the founders Vincent D'Indy's name was also embossed in white block letters. In my need for distraction I took it as a sign. Since I used up my self-allotted mileage already today, tomorrow I would go to the library and start to learn of the man while becoming familiar with the artist.

Vincent D'Indy (1851-1931) was born into an aristocratic family whose ancestral memories would make him a lifelong royalist even while living through several turbulent eras of social revolution and upheaval, when such a stance was if not wrong then at the very least unpopular. His mother died when he was a baby and his grandmother raised him. She was the black sheep of the family having admiration for the republicans and proto forms of socialism such as Saint-Simonism. She was rigid disciplinarian, setting an inflexible schedule for his days with the mantra;

"Have a time for everything and do everything in its time."

This work ethic would remain with him his whole life being part of his general mental makeup along with a stubborn rigidity of thought which was not always to his advantage. Being an amateur musician herself, she taught him piano at an early age. Even this activity, at this point more a hobby, was done with stern regimentation. As an adult D'Indy would give lessons to his own two daughters often bringing them to tears not with cruelness not from raising his voice but by the exacting method of instruction, an incorrect passage was to be played over and over again until executed correctly.

D'Indy's father wanted him to become a lawyer and he himself as a child had ambitions towards a military career. At the age of eight he heard Beethoven's (1770-1827) piano sonatas later claiming that his decision to devote his life to music stems from this day. After professing this decision his musical education became deeper and more formalized. When he was eleven he began studying piano with Louis Diemer and at thirteen: harmony with Albert Lavignac. As his lessons progressed there would also be added on Saturdays piano classes with Antoine François Marmontel. While his musical foundation grew he kept up his law studies too, receiving his baccalaureate.

The year the Prussian war started found him writing his first compositions (1870) *Four Songs Without Words* for piano. With a deep affection for his country and a sense of duty, he volunteered for the army, seeing active duty while leading a bayonet charge at the battle of Val-Fleuri (Dec 16,1870). While still a solider he briefly met composer Cesar Franck (1822-1890). Franck was Belgium born but would spend most of his artistic life based out of Paris even becoming a naturalized citizen. The overall influence he would have on D'Indy's life would be profound and long lasting. Artistically Franck came fully into himself gestating in his own head removed from the influence of trend as he built his foundation off of deep study of Bach and Beethoven melding it with his own ideas and theories. The disregard for the need of any populist bent and the willingness to go outside his nation for composers to draw a template off of would be shared by D'Indy along with a cerebral method of composing music with an architectural logic to it. During his military service, the initial positive response he had received from Franck combined with the usual down time a soldier deals with used for contemplation and scenes of battle where regardless of the cause, life is shown to be cheap, gave D'Indy the resolve to disobey his father and pursue a life in music once his service was over.

Upon leaving the military he would associate with Henri Duparc (1848-1933) who had also been a solider and was now one of Franck's first compositional students. D'Indy renewed his acquaintance with Franck through Duparc, joining a close-knit circle that sat at Franck's feet. D'Indy received support from Franck who spurred him on to study at the conservatory. As a conservatory student there was a disconnect between himself and others at the conservatory which made for a certain degree of isolation. While he suffered under what he saw as an antiquated syllabus there was the reward of his continued interaction with the Franck group in which he was now firmly entrenched.

The acolytes of Franck felt that Rossini and Mendelsohn's music was geared towards populist money making. A similar line with more racially pejorative verbiage would be found in the pamphlets of Richard Wagner (1813-1883) (*Das Juden Thum in der Musik* 1850 originally under a pseudonym republished & expanded under his own name 1869). The Franck group wanted to serve as a counter balance to what they saw as cultural fluff, stressing thought and intelligence in their music. D'Indy would have respite from the rest of the curriculum while auditing classes with Franck (organ class; "Harmonie, Orgue et Composition") but he chaffed under the main curriculum of the conservatory. He helped Franck with the increasingly problematic performance of his composition "La Redemption" which received a cool reception. Upon completion of seeing this project through, D'Indy decided to travel through Germany (1873) not merely as a tourist but to make constructive use of his time soaking in inspiration and adding to his palette. He met Franz Liszt (1811-1886) and

Johannes Brahms (1833-1897) who coldly received him at the door to his country home tersely granting a brief interview. D'Indy would travel all through Germany for several years doing odd jobs to survive. Attending the first Bayreuth Festival (1876) would prove another momentous occasion in D'Indy's life with Wagner becoming the second major influence both intellectually and musically to him.

Two constants in his creative life would be attending the festival which he did every year right up until 1891 and going to his family's country home in Ardeche where he would spend his summers writing. He had an encyclopedic knowledge of the area and would hike the land with friends and family, the ever-present notebook in his pocket ready to record the songs of the shepherds. This inspiration of unadorned nature is in line with the (romantic era) German influence on his art while the appeal of the folk melodies was what he viewed in their unadulterated purity as being artistically linked to the religious vocal and plain song (Renaissance) music that he treasured. In his documenting of the songs of the shepherds could be found his desire at cultural conservatism which he viewed as another aspect of how to best live his life in service of music. An important aspect of his conservationism which transcends the sorted aspects of his later actions was reintroducing the all but forgotten work by Renaissance/Baroque composer Monteverdi's (1567-1643) opera *L'incoronazione di Poppea* (1642-43) with his edition of this opera being the definitive one used.

D'Indy would incorporate aspects of folk songs into his music but he was not looking to bring a folkloric art into his own era; combining it with some new devices while maintaining an authenticity as Bela Bartok (1881-1945) would seek to do. The folk idiom was another component which the logical foundation of his compositions would sometimes utilize.

D'Indy often employed a cyclical form as was also favored by Franck. From Wagner, he pulled the concept of a total art which included multi mediums, all working in concert to contribute to a cohesive whole. Like Wagner he would utilize his pen too, writing about his war experiences and various biographies (Wagner, Franck) and later a multi volume Cours de composition musicale (1903–1905).

To better learn how best to serve his muse he officially became one of Franck's students, an organist at Saint Leu Taverny and an unpaid second timpanist for the new Orchestra of L'Association Artistique de concerts de Chatelet and (organ) prompter from the second performance ever of Bizet's (then) maligned run of *Carmen*. In 1879 D'Indy became chorus master of The Colonne Orchestra. Here he learned via practical application over a four-year period. While at these journeyman jobs he wrote his first symphony which was programmatic, describing various Italian Cities. The symphony was not well received and would be withdrawn from performance as was the fate of some of his other early works such as the comic opera *Attendez Vous-Sous l'Orme* (1882 which outright flopped) and the Symphony "Jean Hungade" (1875).

The muse source materials of Franck, Wagner and his deep knowledge of pre-baroque masters shared some commonalities; the challenge was not how to achieve his own identity but how to combine these things with his own vision so that they coalesced into an organic whole. There were some awards won for pieces written under the strict guidance of Franck but nothing which really "stuck" in regard to lasting in any repertoire. As empowered as he was under the tutelage and as a member of Franck's group there was a sort of stop start rhythm to his artistic ascent as he found a way to envision music attune to his philosophy yet not so self-consciously constructed.

The "Société National de Musique Française" (1871) was founded by Franck, Edouard Lalo (1823-1893), Georges Biszet (1838-1875), Saint-Saëns (1835-1921), Henri Duparc (1848-1933) and Jules Massenet (1842-1912). "Dedicated to the rebirth of a new and more serious French music." Most of these composers under the second empire had been shut out by a system that used favoritism to grant commissions and exposure based almost solely on projected earnings for which safer, commercial works were desired. Post war propaganda by Germany had it that France had lost due to an overly sensual, decadent bent which carried over into the nation's music and intellectual life. It was a sensitive point to this group of composers who wanted to show themselves intellectual and artistic equals. All the members felt that deeper elements of art had been stymied in favor of amusements over true art.

There would be a succession of groups and societies formed over the next several decades. They comprised two main missions, one of (French) cultural promotion and a sort of mutual protection society as lowest common denominator trends in audience expectations were bucked. The problem from the get go with a lot of them was the abstract aspects of if not their mission than how to define certain key aspects. This always led to inner power struggles and a splintering off from the main body to form other groups. The 1880's would find D'Indy achieving artistic success with his fantasy/tone poem hybrid "Symphonie Sur un Chant Montagnard Français" (1887). He would also start to wield more power as he became president of Société Nationale and a member of "Commission Des Auditions Musicales" for the universal exposition of 1889. These universal expositions were of importance for their propaganda in showing other nations both cultural heritage and technological/industrial advances. The expo of 1867 had been important for the arts in retrospect for ignoring or vilifying the body of painters who would go on to become the impressionists and the realist painter Gustav Courbet, who would be defended and promoted in articles by Emil Zola (1840-1902) and more poetically Charles Baudelaire (1821-1867).

There was a dichotomy at play with the official recognition D'Indy was amassing and the ability it granted him to get things done. There was still the struggle against the artistic mores and intergroup fighting to contend with. He was named a Chevalier Legion of Honor the same year he was given an important commission to by Henri Roujon the director of Beaux Arts to help reform the conservatory syllabus. Rather than design a new course or two or build off of the established curriculum D'Indy went far beyond the humble scope of what had been expected of him. The aged professors had become complacent learning how to do their jobs with now minimal amount of effort, the radical overhaul his program suggested offered no appeal to them. A cabal against him was created and he was refused implementation of his plan via denial of funds. When looking back on this attempt D'Indy wryly commented;

"The reports were recognized only to the extent that it was printed at the state's expense only to be promptly buried."

He would refuse to teach or affiliate with the conservatory until changes were made which would not happen until 1912.

One of the reasons why D'Indy's reputation suffers and his work has fallen away from most orchestral repertoires is his moral/intellectual stance. Inherited from his grandmother was a near complete inflexibility in all things. D'Indy lived during a time when France was in a state of near constant dramatic fluctuation. From the fall of Napoleon III, the Paris Commune which morphed into The Third French Republic to The Dreyfus Affair to both world wars. D'Indy in these turbulent times would sometimes find himself on the wrong side of socio/political arguments. This has made D'Indy as both a man and artist in relation to writers akin to the six blind men and the elephant. Was he a young revolutionary wanting to implement serious change to the milieu of Paris's musical society or was he a pedantic reactionary too steeped in tradition and what he saw as a fight against cultural disintegration? He was a little bit of both.

The Société Nationale de Musique was created in 1871. It was founded by Romaine Bussine (1830-1899) and Camille Saint-Saëns. The initial members' roster reads like a who's who of French composers including Franck. The stated mission was to promote the works of living French composers. In the 1880's they began accepting scores from non-French composers but sparingly. There was an inner power struggle With Saint-Saëns leading one side and Franck the other. Franck's side won and upon his death D'Indy was elected president with Saint-Saëns and Bussine both resigning.

The question of what is predominantly French would come up again and again being one of many main points of contention within the many societies D'Indy would be affiliated with. He himself had drawn inspiration from Wagner but felt it did not affect the purity of the "Frenchness" of his music as he transmuted it but the question of dilution was hotly debated. In retrospect, it seems the wrong point of argument, complexity of work not nation of origin should have been the key question. There was, like a lot of other groups a splintering off of the society.

The question of nationalism and purity was brought to head by The Dreyfus Affair (1894-1906) which had far reaching effects and saw almost all artistic and intellectuals polarized to the pro or anti side. D'Indy was on the wrong (anti) side of this argument which would permanently besmirch his reputation well after his death with the more shorthand descriptions of him from this time on merely being "anti-Semitic".

D'Indy's incorrect stance on this issue can not merely be chalked up to racism. The Dreyfus Affair began when a young Jewish artillery officer was accused of spying for Germany, selling secrets to the German embassy. Evidence was manufactured and Dreyfus was accused of treason and sentenced to life imprisonment on Devil's Island in French Guiana. After five years in prison evidence was discovered that the real spy was a commissioned officer Charles Marie Ferdinand Walsin Esterhazy. He was tried but found innocent as the military high command thought a guilty verdict for him at this late date would besmirch the entire high command. The high command then compounded its mistake by trying to cover up Esterhazy's activities and manufacturing further evidence against Dreyfus. Emil Zola would publish an open letter "J'Accuse" (1898) in the paper L'Aurore addressed to French President Felix Faure. In this letter, he accuses the government of anti-Semitism and the wrongful imprisonment of Alfred Dreyfus.

Anti-Semitism was a real problem but the Dreyfus Affair became a spring board to question and challenge other social and political issues. As the affair went on it came to also embody the question of the social contract and tradition versus progress. When the affair came to the nation's consciousness D'Indy was at the apex of his career. His past experiences witnessing how composers who did not want to compromise were treated in the corridors of power probably played a factor in his not being too enthusiastic about a deluge washing away the power he had with which he sought to do good. A lot of the pro-Dreyfusists in the arts communities were intellectuals which was often a byword for atheists. Also, a lot of intellectuals believed in various forms of (proto) socialism (Saint-Simonism et al) which did not sit well with D'Indy who was a monarchist having been born into an aristocratic family.

From his time of military service on he had always had a nationalistic streak in him which combined with his religious convictions and natural inclinations made him closed off to any discussions of cultural flexibility. Like the artistic feuds D'Indy had found himself often caught up in, not everyone he had to align himself with had the same motives. But a common *enemy* made for strange bedfellows in this case to the detriment of the future perception for the composer.

From the publication of Zola's letter on the world started to watch. Stances and reasons needed to be articulated. During this cultural civil war, there would be a pro and anti-manifesto issued which almost all the major players of Parisian cultural and artistic society would sign. "Dreyfusists" were those immersed in deep debate and thought, trying to start a dialogue about French society and social injustices. The pro Dreyfus leaders were Zola, Anatole France (who would read a funeral oration at Zola's funeral which was delayed as a direct result of the affair) (1844-1924) and Marcel Proust (1871-1922). The anti Dreyfus manifesto was circulated by "Nationalist Ligue de la Partie Française" with D'Indy being the prime mover behind it, also garnering among its collected signatures those of Augusta Holmes who was the director of the comic opera, Albert Carre, critic Henri Gauthier-Villars, Pierre de Breville, Professor of music history at the Paris conservatory Louis Bougault-Ducoudray. There was also a third far smaller party; "Comité de l'Appel à l'Union" which ostensibly wanted the two parties to reconcile, made up of Claude Debussy (1862-1918), Gustave Charpentier (1860-1956), music historian Julien Tiersot (1857-1936) and conductor Edouard Colonne (1838-1910). Saint-Saëns believed that Dreyfus was innocent but had several generals in his family and so deferred from signing anything.

An artist's stance is sometimes over simplified to "Those who had official power and recognition were traditionalist that wanted to retain their place. Those outside of the system wanted to break up tradition and the established order" but often motive even for those in bad faith was more complex. D'Indy's stance never changed but put him on different sides of the fence throughout his life. This fluctuation of the righteousness of his side is a main contributor to the rise and fall of his reputation.

A positive to arise from this social upheaval during the Dreyfus Affair was the creation of The Schola Cantorum (1894). Initially the Schola Cantorum was a society for promotion and teaching of religious music, especially Gregorian chant. It was inspired in part by the performing group "Les Chanteurs de Saint-Gervais" (1892) which was founded by the concert master of Saint Gervais, Charles Bordes (1863-1909). The Shola was the collaboration between Bordes, D'Indy and Alexandre Guilmant (1837-

1911).

The Dreyfus Affair had made D'Indy resolved to fuse his art and politics. He wanted to defend and promote traditional culture which while with a conservative sounding tinge to it was not necessarily outright sinister. D'Indy would utilize concepts that he had originally designed for the conservatory. From the banning of the church and its music during the French Revolution (1789-1799) there had been, to different degrees, a marginalization of religious music and its training which persisted right up into D'Indy's day. Even as the Schola was being formed the government was merely trickling out funds for only six schools for the entire state. To ensure their own autonomy and not risk being closed if state funds dried up, the Schola ran off of donations and from tuition fees. While the foundation of the program was solidly traditional, D'Indy could respect any compositional student so long as they were serious in their approach and resolve.

The Dreyfus Affair ended with neither side being fully appeased. This was accepted out of necessity of restoring social order. Many important cultural and political questions remained unresolved and would rise to the fore again as subject of discourse over the next few decades. For D'Indy, there was never any kind of philosophical about face. Instead he seems to have decided his cultural battle was best fought via the teachings coming out of The Schola. He was still conservative in his thought and much like his grandmother had been with him and he with his daughters, his pedantic method of teaching did not change with the times.

D'Indy felt that to compose music, no matter how powerful was not enough. He had a compulsion to serve art and his fellow artist. While involved with The Schola D'Indy kept up activities as President of the society. The inner group struggles continued over question of programing causing Maurice Ravel (1875-1937) to break off to form Société de Musique Indépendente (1909). This group would include many of the younger generation of composers and would offer a deeper sense of freedom in what would be promoted feeling the more political aspects of music a moot point.

D'Indy who had once had to battle the refusal of the conservatory to evolve now found himself on the other side of a similar argument.

Ravel's group wanted freedom of not just nation but also musical era as well, as exemplified by their first concert season which included works by Ravel but also harpsichord music by English composer Henry Purcell (1659-1695).

During the First World War, there was another swell of nationalism in the art world which caused a rift among many composers. Despite having been inspired by Wagner, D'Indy started (1916) "Ligue Nationale Pour la Defense de la Musique Française" whose goal was to emphasize only the purest French music. Music of Wagner and other German composers was proscribed during this time. Ravel and his former teacher Faure refused to join as they felt artistic isolation for any nation would lead to stagnation. Even non-politicized artists, dealers and gallerists not of French origin suffered a cultural apartheid. Practical considerations saw Faure/Ravel's group merge with D'Indy's (1915). It was a turbulent partnership which did not last, things coming to a head when, with their limited budget D'Indy had to cut most of the chamber music series which effected the newly merged fraction of the group more than his own.

After the First World War, the Schola had established a power base forming a union with the "idea of promoting an exchange of views among colleagues." While D'Indy was to remain rigid in his instruction, this along with concert performances which featured diverse programs that included Bach's "B Minor Mass", Monteverdi's *L'Incoronaonie*, Gluck's *Orphée* showed if not the lessening of importance of the fear of cultural erosion from art originating outside the nation then a greater flexibility.

There would be continued debate on France's cultural heritage, the preservation and evolution of it. Xenophobia and anti-Semitism would remain in varying degrees but with the rise of fascism during the Second World War it often became easier to separate the verbiage of debate on cultural preservation of those who were thinking merely in terms of art for art's sake rather than the agenda of art as propaganda, the purely intellectual versus the socio-political.

D'Indy's wife had died in 1905. At the time, it was not common and despite being constantly labeled as a reactionary he had treated her as an equal, depending upon her counsel. In 1920 he met Caroline Janson in a brasserie in Montparnasse. Even though he was thirty-six years older than her, they married. The memory of his first wife compounded with that of his daughter Berthe who had died in 1913 made him spend less time in Ardeche and more in the Cote d 'Azur. He built a villa in there for his new wife and himself where they could vacation and he write. The villa in Agay was on the ocean. The view, his new wife and the warmth of the Mediterranean sun was conducive to his work. With his piano quintet (OP 81 1924) he wrote his first chamber work in twenty years. Before 1920 he had preferred shorter melodies including this preference in his teachings. In his late period, he adopted longer flowing ones for his chamber pieces. In this final period he seems to have let emotion meld with the cerebral. Whether age made it so that he had to mete out where his energy went or he loosened up his philosophy, his last period while slowed down production wise shows some added influences in his palette along with the ones which he had utilized his entire life.

Politics aside, another reason that D'Indy's music has fallen to the wayside is that it does not embody any extreme. His tone poem/programmatic music was meticulously constructed yet it lacked the outright fire of his romantic era forerunners who had invented the genre. Neither did he mix in innovation to such a degree as Debussy or Ravel.

It still makes for enjoyable listening, especially his late period works. The late works retain his usual level of control while allowing for some new coloration to creep in too. Post-World War One there would be moments of the new schools of composers lapsing into a neo classicism (Stravinsky, Ravel et al) and while these compositions which contained those elements were not necessarily overall embraced neither did they seem to be met with as much indifference or criticism as D'Indy's music which more often than not embraced aspects of it, especially in the years immediately following his death which saw the true dropping off of visibility of his work. As a point of comparison; D'Indy's *Diptyque Méditerranéen Pour Orchestra* (1926) which was inspired by his new summer work home and Debussy's "La Mer" (1903). Debussy wrote his poem to the ocean far from it, calling upon memories of its emotional effects, impressions truer than reality for being recreated in his head from Burgundy, in structure and finish, less abstract than other of his compositions. If Debussy's ocean is a walk along an untamed sunlit shore bordered by cypress crowned cliffs, then D'Indy's is the same view from the balcony of a villa out onto the bay. Although not by any means an artistic dialogue between the two artists, Debussy would use more traditional compositional devices than was his want whereas D'Indy would put aside some of his more cerebral in favor of the more emotional. Both tackling the same subject described occasionally with similar words yet different cadence. Yet, Debussy's poem is still a staple of the modern repertoire.

D'Indy had once said "An artist can expect nothing from the present. He knows that his mission is to serve, an artist should be inspired by a splendid charity." He had given his all, a lifetime of service to his muse using every tool available. Unfortunately, in his earnestness to serve he employed rhetoric which over the course of time morphed into dogma. Future generations would have trouble separating the scores from the words. Each generation of young lions seeks to supplant the previous generations who themselves, once revolutionaries, settled into "the establishment". The time between the two world wars there would be plenty of manifestos articulating the mission of each group (Second Viennese School, Futurism, Dadaist, and Surrealism). Even when a group's rhetoric was strong none were as unbending to change as D'Indy would prove to be.

The question becomes how much can and should one separate bad behavior of an artist from their work? And are there degrees of bad behavior with some, towards women or one's peers, more acceptable than those which are political in nature. D'Indy had a nationalist streak in him which put him on the wrong side of arguments in his quest to preserve and promote culture. Although xenophobia and anti-Semitism had been around pre-Dreyfus Affair, after the First World War it was easier for those whose cultural concerns were not steeped in bias or hatred to separate their cause from those with a different agenda but who tried to utilize a similar verbiage. Memories blur and D'Indy with his nationalistic streak is often lumped in with the bad that came after, a man who was unbending having had his reputation effected by (social) change. Unfettered from the dogma in a way the he himself could never be, D'Indy's music offers up pleasure, the perfect soundtrack to daydreams.

I walk through the far end of the Luxembourg Gardens, down one of the tree lined paths. Briefly I look up, there is a lilting grace to the sun strobing between the swaying leaves of the canopy. I hum to myself but stop as I think back. The last night, I had gone over to make sure everything was set. She went over the train timetables as I stood by the window looking out, rolling the empty shot glass between the palms of my hand. The bottom of the glass, octagonal and beveled, each time ridge hits flesh switching gears into new thought.

I had put things in motion but it would have happened anyways just perhaps a little slower. I am feeling somewhat better but still must make sure not to wear myself out. Each day I walk a little bit longer than the previous day. I pick up what I need from the market and head home. I put my hat on the table hole side up as I had been sweating. I empty my pockets into the dish on the night table. I keep a pen in my shirt pocket in the way people wear religious medallions

.

ITALIAN RIVER FLOWS

I cut myself on her lips, the debris of a glass sculpture so pale as to almost be camouflaged to the naked eye, someone having accidently bumped into it, knocking it upon the floor where it smashes. Now these shards have drawn blood from me. Go to sleep, go to sleep it is nothing, non e nulla.

Almost the size of another person, the silhouette of rumpled sheets besides me, evidence of scattered thoughts and the morning's blues. I was the writer, the boyfriend, the no-good bastard. By which name I was referred to did not depend upon my current activity but by others perception of me at any given time.

Even though there was a pall over the city, I already knew how much I was going to miss it. I did my best thinking in the shower and on my walks. Soon I would be somewhere else and on those future walks when not actively working on a piece my mind would turn back, acute memory once again wandering these temporarily abandoned streets.

The goodbyes, the flight everything unpleasant blurred into an abstraction that my mind tried to push into the back behind trivia and rarely made recipes. I had jet lag so it took me a few days to notice that the only blanket which was long enough to cover my entire body was quilted with rough threaded seams. Here and there the stitching stuck up, late at night jabbing and poking so that half asleep, there was the feeling of small things biting or crawling across one's body.

As always, I have my music but I wait to play any of it. There is that delicious torture akin to trying to keep a secret in or not to come. There is Don Byas who reminds me of all the little side streets that I should be walking down as I make my way to The Jardin des Plantes to sketch or some other regular haunt. There is Lester Young who is cloud like and in his later period, possessing that fragile crumbling beauty and who regardless of the song always reminds me of us. Music though is my main source of inspiration and I can only avoid the ache of ghosts for so long.

I had come, knowing that it was important but in an abstract way. The pliancy of honesty, everyone whom I was temporarily leaving kept telling me that I would not like it nor have fun, I was reminded that the people whose company I treasured had moved or died. Those who I would find time to visit once stateside told me of the bars and restaurants I used to like and assured me that they had not changed. Both groups were right. When Cecilia asked me to explain why I had to make the trip, the best I could articulate was that I had to renew my inner strength with struggle, putting myself in less than ideal situations where not every detail was as I like it.

It seemed to rain the entire time. I lived within site of the ocean and often walked the beach. Bad weather aside, the beach was not crowded as it was not the type where one would lay down a blanket to sprawl on between swimming and participating in other such activities as one imagines doing on a beach in California. Nature still owned this particular spot and she constantly reminded all by the booming voice of her waves hitting the sharp fingered crags of rocks which poked up from the water, the pumiced roughness of the sand which I could not imagine walking on barefoot and the vastness of the tree topped cliffs which overlooked the beach further shrinking down any humans who bothered to come. A few times I spotted yellow slickered fishermen standing in the surf with their rods. I stopped to briefly chat, something unseen loudly splashing around in the large white bucket by their side.

I was miserable but not unhappy if you can understand the subtle differences. A few times I popped into the city, there were a few places to drink but not the endless choices or variety as could be found back in my arrondissement. The rain never let up and as I walked the once familiar streets it added to the effect of feeling like my own ghost. I poked around one of the few remaining independent bookstores. Whenever I travel there are certain things regardless of my destination that I must bring, sketchpad, notebook and something to read. Even with my longer journeys I always pack so that it is carry-on as by the time I get to where I am going I do not then want to have to wait for my luggage to do a lap on the carousel. I apply a faulty logic with what book I bring with me, always taking one the size of a paperback as I do not want to overstuff my suitcase with a big book. But I finish it during my trip and end up having to get at least one more if not as on longer trips several. All the smaller books take up more space than one larger book would. I tell myself that I will leave a few of the books behind but I can never let myself do that and the few times I tried, I regretted it and then bought another copy at home but it was then not the same, the new copy in my hand was not the one I read as ambient street noise of Livorno drifted in through the window late at night getting softer and softer until right before dawn vanishing.

I grab a thick tome by Ignazio Silone the size of an unabridged dictionary. I was in a rare can't lose situation, if I ended up not liking the book, then I would not have to lug it back with me, if it did appeal to me then I discovered something else which to enjoy. Of course I ended up liking it. The physicality of the book too was a sort of comfort. Although it dominated the space in my book bag, I brought it out with me on my walks and sorties into the city.

It turns out that the Silone book I bought was actually three novels gathered under one cover by Steerforth Press (The best Italian into English translations of modern Italian literature). *The Abruzzo Trilogy* is a slight variation on a genre which has somewhat been in flux since its inception due to artistic evolution and misuse of the term.

Romain Rolland (1866-1944) wrote essays, literary criticisms, novels and historical tracts. His important non-fiction was diverse, from treatises on humanist theater to pre-baroque lyric opera to Gandhi (1869). His writings on Gandhi essentially introduced him to a non-specialized audience in the West (1916) and the two actually met later in 1931. It is almost a misnomer to say, "He is best known for..." as despite winning the Nobel Prize for literature (1915) he is largely with the exception of bookworms and special field academicians, unknown in the United States. However, one aspect of his oeuvre, even if unknown, would have influence on modern literature right up to this day.

Jean Christophe (1904-1912) was a ten-volume cycle of novels. It depicts the entire life trajectory of the same named German musician/composer from cradle to grave. Before this, other authors had series of novels that were thematically linked but there were differences from what came before and the way that Rolland evolved the form. Linking him to his literary forefathers (Emil Zola 1840-1902, Honoré Balzac 1799-1850) was that like both of them his novels in the cycle were all interconnected to form one great whole. From Zola he absorbed the technique of showing the cross sections of society. Roland was not an acolyte nor even a particular fan of the Zola formed "Naturalists" (realists) school of writing but he did borrow some devices from him for use as a descriptive device. Roland considered his novels musical and with the characters motivations dictated by emotions and not just serving as needed devices to move the narrative in a desired direction as was usually the case with the classic novels. In writing about *Jean Christophe,* he said that to him, the novel *flowed like a river* and the term Roman-Fleuve was coined to describe a genre.

The Roman-Fleuve genre is said to have started with Romain Rolland with some components of the genre mined from his peers and near contemporaries. In the most basic definition a Roman-Fleuve is a multi-volume work with each part having its own title and the work overall encompassing an epoch. The author of such a cycle works in their thoughts on society and culture and more often than not some sort of dynastic line is followed via one if not all the characters.

An often-cited example of this genre is Marcel Proust's (1871-1922) *A Le Recherché Du Temp Perdu* (in French, 7 volumes 1913-1927). Arguably this meets all the genre's criteria and it could seem splitting hairs to point out that the cycle's observation on the sociopolitical mores are all presented as not time moving forward or the steady stream of history but merely as smaller occurrences as remarked upon in the solipsist views of the narrator "Marcel", time and history as the canvas he paints a self-portrait upon rather than including his figure in that of a larger picture.

Men of Goodwill (27 volumes in French 1932-1946) by Jules Romains (1885-1972) meets some of the Roman-Fleuve criteria and in ways is the reverse of Proust's opus. Where Proust concentrates more on the "I" of the narrator and two upper crust families he is connected to, Jules's vast work has no family lineage to serve as its center but offers an intricate mosaic of French society. Having been a great fan of Tolstoy's (1828-1910) *War and Peace* this work encompasses a huge cast of characters from all walks of life, the entire narrative flowing from October 6, 1908 until October 7, 1933. Proust's work is told with use of intricate rhythms ping ponging between the current time of the narrator, his past and then the past of some of his other characters as related to him by anecdote or ease dropping. *Men..* unfolds in linear time fashion but stylistically has variations in it, a thing which would later but done for the much shorter work *Exercises in Style* (1947) by Raymond Queneau.

The man who would become Ignazio Silone (1900-1978) was born Secondo Tranquili in Pescina (Abruzzo Region of Italy). His father died when he was eleven. His mother took up weaving to earn a meager living for her family which aside from Secondo included his five siblings, after the death of her husband. In 1915 the Avezzano Earthquake killed over thirty thousand people including Secondo's mother. The earthquake also destroyed the family's finances. Out of all his siblings only one brother also survived the earthquake and childhood illness. He and his brother were sent to live with his maternal grandmother.

With no clear-cut feeling of purpose, he wandered around awhile before finally finishing secondary school in 1917. He started working with socialist groups and became a leader in the anti-war movement and an editor of the Roman Socialist paper *Avanguardia*. At the young age of 21 (1921), he became a covert leader for the Italian Communist Party (PCI) whose inception he helped with. One of his main roles at this time was in helping to set up and facilitate cells (secretly) in Spain and France. He also furthered the cause by becoming editor of *Il Lavoratore* (The Worker) in Trieste (1922). His vocation made him use many aliases for both his and his allies' protection. One of these thought up while in a Spanish jail "Ignazio Silone" would become the second skin never shed.

In 1928, his brother Romolo would be jailed for his party activities and would eventually die from mistreatment while being held by the fascists. Aspects of his brother's imprisonment and torture are said to have served as inspiration in his later writings but not as is sometimes said as the entire makeup of any one particular figure. Later in life Ignazio would say his brother was well educated but only "vaguely political".

Ignazio would be sent in an official capacity to the Soviet Union for a congress. During this time (1929-30) there was much debate about the direction the communist party was moving in under the overall direction of Stalin. During debates which would ultimately prove irrelevant, he found himself moving more and more towards an anti-Stalin stance not necessarily realizing that it could not now be separated from the party over which his control had basically become total. Among other things which he found disheartening was how Russia first centralized all the smaller groups throughout Europe then dictated policy not making any allowance for variations which were relevant for each country/location/people. His stance would initially get him suspended from the central committee in 1930 and then a year later, expelled altogether.

After his expulsion, he moved to Switzerland seeking out psychoanalysis and treatment for TB and major depression in a sanitarium. It is during his time in the sanitarium he initially took up the pen to write fiction. His first novel *Fontamara* was published in Zurich in 1930 (in English 1934). It resulted in international fame, being translated into twenty-seven languages. Despite its popularity and social relevance, it could not be translated into his native Italian because of its anti-fascist stance.

From his own poverty-stricken beginnings Ignazio would always be concerned with the plight of the lower working class especially from his native region. His first novel revolved around the farmers ("cafoni") dealing with the power and policy of the fascist regime. There is a little bit of the traditional narrative devices of a writer running into three travelers in the middle of emigrating from their home who tell their story, the in-book author deciding to make their story into a novel. The novel alternates between the point of view of the three narrators; Giuva who is an out of work farmer that is ashamed of his position and does not want conflict but only to work. He is aware of the injustices being done upon his village but still holds out hope that to not make waves, things will eventually go back to how they had been. There is Matala, who is his wife. She is more abstractly idealistic and does not as easily hold her tongue or actions; she is one of the women who walk to Rome to protest one of the many injustices over the course of the narrative. Their son who is only ever known as "the child" is the last of the three narrators. The novel is written in the social realist vein and although dormant, hope is eluded to in that the child and other youth admire the dissenters. The axis to a lot of the action moves upon the character of Berardo Viola whose family is from the village but had been a soldier and received some formal education too. He becomes the spokesmen for the village and in some ways is the symbol of their plight in that he seems to have no luck but bad. Berardo is somewhat worldlier than his fellow villagers trying to organize rebellion but despite a better understanding of what is going on, ultimately for all his righteous dissent he is buried under the weight of the fascist machinery. The novel's tempo once the narration device is set up builds up tension through a series of incidents, each becoming worse than that preceding it. Message and metaphor aside, the most basic explanation of the novels synopsis is the power of the fascist regime on a remote village of poor farmers. They had, even during the pre-fascist regime never had use for abstract thoughts and ideas, their lives locked into the practical harmony of earth and season. The new government and all its edicts hold no meaning for them and are more often than not, incomprehensible. The moneyed landowners sympathetic to the new government set about systematically fleecing the cafoni, never to the point of absolute ruin as they must be allowed to carry on as to keep providing.

Silone's next two novels were directly connected with some of the characters moving from one novel to the next. *Bread and Wine* (1936) takes place in the same region as the previous book. The narrative device differs though from his first novel. This novel and *The Seed Beneath the Snow* which was written concurrent with its predecessor focus on Pietro Spina an anti-fascist with a good formal education. Prior to the book's opening he has been on the run through Europe from fascist. In ill health and still a wanted man he returns to Italy and is helped to disguise himself as a priest adopting the identity of Paulo Spada.

Spada makes his way to a remote village, from the very start while enroot he is disguised as a priest but does not want to play the part, however starting with an incident at an inn he is forced more and more to take on that very role. With his socialist sympathies and Christian morals Spada represents the spiritual questing of the author himself as he tried to reconcile two seemingly divergent ways of thinking into a goodness the transcended dogma and political parties and could be given practical application in everyday life. Like the cafoni of his first novel these farmers too have very little use for abstract thought. If what he had witnessed before fleeing to Switzerland fueled some of the first novel, then in the second and third novel could be added to that his frustration and disillusionment of other political parties and their infighting and the cowardly actions taken by average nonpolitical citizens for self-preservation. The cafoni still largely do not understand the current political climate in Italy and their ignorance in these novels is seen less as a victimology as in the first and more as a form of collusion. The final novel of the trilogy has some points which lapse into political pedagogical tracts.

Although the first book character wise is not directly connected to the other two, thematically the all are united by sharing some important aspects, the mental and spiritual make up of a specific section of people at a defined point in time. The first book could almost serve as a prelude or the dark clouds which herald an oncoming storm. The difference in the two more politically aware main characters of Viola and Spina in the novels is an interesting study in intellectual contrasts. Spina is less intellectually passive. He wants to inset himself into the possibility of history, not just fermenting revolution against what he views as a wrong way but desiring to do all he can after the fact to help bring about a new way. Both characters have "pure" motives but where Viola is thwarted more by bad luck and the sheer scope of his opposition, Spina fails by the sometimes unintentional betrayals of the very people he is working for. In the end with his death he does not seek to redeem them but to underline his own purity.

Even during their initial release these books contained so many powerful messages that the U.S Army bootlegged *Fontamara* and *Bread and Wine*, handing them out to Italians during the liberation of Italy (1943). After the war Ignazio returned to Italy and the political arena as leader of the Democratic Socialist Party. In 1950 he retired devote himself solely to writing.

The trilogy of novels and a lot of his life's work was anti-fascist but not merely an artistic mission of opposition. There was the desire for freedom but a particular type of freedom that would allow for enlightenment via an everyday decency. He had absorbed himself into different groups; socialism, communism and Christianity. It was not that he was a dilettante but each mode of thought/action was either too rigid in their system of philosophy or moved too far beyond their initial conception which had held its appeal for him. The Abruzzo Trilogy does not meet all the requirements to formally be of the roman-fleuve genre although it comes very close. With groups of characters and sometimes multiple narrators all three books are still pretty straight ahead in their trajectory with no non-linear digressions. Presented over the course of the three novels are varying social strata of a people during the fascists years. There is the anguish of not being able to overcome evil despite what fairy tales had led us to believe and the realization that sometimes evil is fostered unintentionally by the very people whom it preys upon.

Sometimes referred to as an Italian Proust, Andrea Giovene (1904-1995) wrote a sweeping epic simply called (in English), after its main character *Sansevero* (1966-1970). The cycle is five volumes long being put into two books with the first (in English) being the first three. The comparison with Proust is somewhat inaccurate, both are of the same genre and both to some extent family sagas but as told through the "I" of a main protagonist. The rhythm and tense of the narrator Proust employs is eschewed by Andrea in favor of a more linear and first-person method. With Proust, one is aware of outside events of society so much as they effect or are noticed by Marcel whereas Andrea's main character Giuliano Sansevero is full engaged, we witness the story starting from when he is a little boy as he grows whereas with Proust's Marcel it is more episodic as we swim the stream of his memories and not that of history.

Although Andrea's rhythm is more a straight forward one, an intricacy is achieved in how thematic aspects of the cycle slowly morphs without ever full shedding the previous theme. The start of the book and the thing which really connects it to *The Abruzzo Trilogy* is its initial theme. In real life Andrea was born into an ancient titled Italian family in the section of society that would see itself left largely with the choice of extinction of collaboration with the fascists. The start of the cycle shows the titled being if not dragged into the modern age actively, then confronted with new ways in which power is obtained and wielded, previously unimagined as no lineage is involved in the process. Even as the beachhead established in the socio-political arena by the fascists grows, ancient bloodlines and family names offer up some protection serving as a crumbling shield. Despite how outmoded noblesse oblige increasingly seem, to the older generation they are reminder of past glory not just of the lineage but the country itself even as it also serves as a sort of cancer, eating away at already dwindling family fortunes to those who refuse to adapt and form a symbiosis with the new government.

The sections are all given titles whose meanings are often apparent by the sections' end. The first part shows a combination of Giuliano's father's folly in putting money into social ritual no longer totally necessary nor meaningful, such as balls, banquets physically restoring and expanding the family estate, working in concert with a new age whose code of honor in business and politics which if not completely absent then drastically different. It mirrors some the themes of *The Abruzzo Trilogy*, only it shows the view from a different stratum of society.

While the cycle shows what life in Italy is like under the Fascist regime, it is not solely concerned with that, the politics being merely one of many components. There is a large cast of characters with very few remaining throughout the entire cycle. What makes it easier to keep track who is who and what happens to them is more often than not once a character leaves the section they are in, they may be referred to again but do not come back. A lot of the characters serve as sort of symbols or metaphors for types of thought/thought put into action but they are not static, it is not a throwback to older literature where someone was *bad* because that is how they needed to be for the narrative. Even with the characters who serve to symbolize something, it is done organically and they represent a thought or manner of living because of the place and time they inhabit not merely to serve as device. Throughout the work knowledge of metaphor/symbolism can add a layer of depth and enjoyment but over analyzing the symbolism regardless of accuracy can also become a distraction lessoning the overall experience such as sometimes happens to people reading Thomas Mann's *Magic Mountain*.

The cycle slowly morphs, at the most basic level, there is the story of a young boy becoming a man as tempered by his era, although executed in a way that is not as maudlin as that sounds. Then the last part of the first book becomes almost a pastoral with slowly darkening underpinnings. The overall narrative has a sense of forward thrust; the main character even as he is out in the world searching for the meaning to himself in his own thoughts is also in the stream of life. The sections do not have major stylistic changes but the themes change while not minimizing those of its predecessor but building upon them. It manages to be both epic but also personal, helped by witnessing Giuliano's growth which comes about via outward catalyst and his own introspections.

From his familial home where he lives in a sort of floating library apart from the others to the seminary school to his first place in a working-class neighborhood (Milan) to his military service (Ferrara) et al the cycle's inner rhythm falls into a pattern of Giuliano living someplace, becoming absorbed into the life of his environment some of which often goes against his nature for which he is offered up further knowledge via his observations and participations. He often finds that due to a time table not his own but propelled by happenstance or fate he must move on. None of the places he stays are outright *bad* as that would devolve the story to the level of a Balzacian pot-boiler. He manages to establish meditative ritual in all of his surroundings where reflections of what he is going through serve as a sort of incubator. Another strength of the cycle is there is no sense of third person detachment as what he sees and muses over is related to us including his own faults too. With some situations; be it a first love or later the married woman with whom he carries out an affair while doing his military service his stoicism is mixed with a sort of dark absurdist humor. He is often well aware that some of the problems he faces are by his own design yet even when acutely feeling the repercussions emotionally, there is never that sense of any absolute where he will fall to his knees head thrown back beating on his chest with clenched fists.

Giuliano is an appealing character, it is not merely the plot and descriptive intricacies which keep one invested in the cycle's progression but the well-rounded protagonists. Part of this is the character's mental makeup. From when we are first introduced to him as a youth he is older than his age but never precocious. It is not artificial nor is it the older version of Giuliano transposing his current sensibilities onto the younger him of the narrative's start as there are still some youthful (teenage) aspects to him present before he leaves his familial home for the first time to go to school.

From when he first leaves home he takes himself seriously but does not view things such as affairs of the heart or the dissolution of his once proud and well to do family as a matter of life or death. He feels the pangs to varying degrees but like the narrative itself, continues to move forward. In some ways Giuliano represents the intellectual potential of what good may eventually come from this new age as his system of thought is built off of an appreciation of some of the intellectual and spiritual thinkers who had come before him and to which he grafts on new possibilities as gleaned by his life experiences in a country whose social mores were in flux.

A personal favorite section of the cycle for me is from the first book, *The Devil*. As this section starts Giuliano is twenty-six years old and finds himself in Rome. All the places he has lived and his ever-changing life, he feels all the miles under him but there is no sense of fatigue or of having frittered away his time despite a seeming lack of practical skills which would lead to a fulfilling traditionally structured life. He initially is living in an attic room, often shorthand for poverty stricken-bohemianism, in the seedy Hotel Colonna. The hotel owner Hans Tenca is painted as intelligent even forward thinking but with vices which he nurtures as if virtues and hidden only so much as to pass a cursory inspection of his personality. He goes out of his way to talk with Giuliano, often sharing his fascination with horrific crimes, which he narrates in a flat voice "As if they were part of some tourist itinerary". After each account Hans would then grow silent waiting for some kind of response from Giuliano who instinctually remained non-committal, neither relishing nor disapproving of anything he heard. In this way, he passed a sort of secret test which then allows Hans to offer introduction to friends of his whom he assures will enjoy his company.

There is a semblance of a mirrored echoing effect all throughout the section. This new crowd all live in "The Grilli Palace" owned by Palo Grilli. Palo's family was of Papal nobility, their power and wealth was not derived from an ancient bloodline but through finance and patronage of the arts which only went back a generation or two. For most of his early life Palo had been under the thumb of his controlling mother via her regency of the family fortune right up until he was twenty-six, when Palo's mother and father died, one shortly after the other. Palo inherited a large fortune and had only one sibling, a sister who initially is going to go to a convent, to share it with. The family lawyer courts her more out of the appeal of her finances than anything else she has to offer. Palo is given an allowance and the enormous family estate "The Grilli Palace". He then decided to pursue a life of decadence to compensate for all the years of the overly measured existence he had lived under his mother. Palo is older than Giuliano but both men started to emerge from a sort of intellectual/spiritual gestation at the same age albeit with drastically different ambitions. Their initial connection is one of the goal of self-discovery but using different methods.

Giuliano moves into The Grilli Palace. Throughout the city Palo has a reputation as a decadent sensualist, only a certain type socializes with him and then at their own risk. Besides Giuliano, there are already encamped in the palace several other eccentric borders and a constant nightly floating card game. In some ways Palo is akin to a less solitary, less mechanized version of Jean Des Esseintes from J.K Huysmans's (1848-1907) *Against Nature* (1884). There is a series of discourses between Palo and Giuliano occurring over the course of the section and often in the midst of the action that show not only the difference in their development but a contrast in how they pursue knowledge and process it into their personal philosophy. Palo prefers to think up sociological experiments which allow for him to indulge appetite and then work the results and observations into his philosophy whereas Giuliano has a preexisting way of thinking and after a situation is over contemplates it and see if anything which he learned can be added to his knowledge. Palo represents a sort of freedom from morality but is not all advanced (modern) thought, as he does sometimes enjoy perversity for merely its own sake.

Despite both being thinkers, it becomes more and more apparent that the two of them will find no common ground. Money becomes tighter and tighter for Palo who not only spends freely but often does not charge his interesting borders much rent. There is a vast library of rare volumes which symbolically is slowly cannibalized along with its actual shelving.

Speeding up the tempo of his ruin is his brother in law outmaneuvering him with a density of accounting and leasing papers. In a slow steady stream all the borders go into various forms of exile. Finally the estate is *leased* to industrialists from Lombardy who throw lavish balls every week attended by the collaborating rich and the upper echelon of the fascist party. Although with none of the initial nobility or even concrete sense of purpose, Palo's downfall via financial ruin through trickery resembles aspects of Giuliano's father's fate. Palo and Giuliano could be said to be aspects of two paths along one road, a point underlined by Palo eventually ending up having to live alone in the hot attic room from which Giuliano had initially departed to join him. This section has a sense of dark, churning wonderment and could be seen as akin to a scherzo movement of a Mahler symphony which will be followed by a slower moving lushness.

Both cycles reinsert humanity into history which so often with the passage of time becomes reduced down to lists of names, dates and numbers. Neither cycle should be viewed merely as *war novels*. The fascists elements in each cycle are important factors but one of many components. Regardless of one's knowledge of history in which each cycle occurs, they can both be enjoyed as great works of art.

I write to Cecilia that I will be returning shortly. I could have called, it is not that I want to stay here but in saying out loud all the timetables etc. to which I will temporarily have to adhere there is a risk of inertia setting in and freezing me to the spot no matter how badly I want to return home.

I take one more walk on the beach. I am leaving America, again. We do not need nor understand each other any longer. Ah do not look at me that way, it is not you, it is me baby. I have to go; now novelty and cleverness is valued over intelligence. I am speaking in the broadest terms of course but the horror of it for me is that I feel justified in doing so.

My feet crunch on the hard sand, I zip my jacket all the way up. Sepia lighting off of the bay, the sky meets the sea as one seemingly endless body whose flesh is goose pimpled with rain.

PARIS PRINTS: GERICAULT & IDEM PARIS

I flicked on the light and waited for it to warm up so that I could get a good shave. I rested my razor on the lip of the sink much in the same way I did my paint brushes. I had some wash pieces which I wanted to execute before the daylight waned into that mellow gold whisper which describes the encroaching night and a new potential collector interested strictly in my drawings, as he made it a point to tell me three times, whom I had to meet for drinks at Melinda's later. My eyes wandered the circuit of the room as I waited. There was blood on the floor. No, it was just the grain of the wood as seen in the stuttering fluorescents. Still, summer is gone.

I got some good work done; the entire afternoon spent watching my hand create pieces of life on paper as Mozart's clarinet concertos kept my self-imposed solitude a thing of joy. I was just able to run home to clean up before my appointment. I went out on my little balcony to check the temperature as my haste in getting home had kept me too heated to accurately gauge. Off in the distance was the minaret by Café de la Mosquée de Paris. It was cool out. Even higher up, the air was still. The smoke coming from each home lingered. Each above its chimney where the cold air further bunched it, white flowers resting upon stems of orange clay or dull iron, blooming all across the left bank.

I got there about five minutes early just so that I could say hello to everybody instead of merely nodding as I walked by. A friendliness befitting one of my favorite places to catch a drink or hold a meeting, especially now that Olivier was gone. The collector showed up on time. Living with portents, he did not feel the need as did so many who made their money in the business world of flexing his muscle by having made me wait. We shook hands.

We chatted. Michael had made his money by starting a laundry service that within a very short amount of time handled all the tourists' hotels on the right bank. After a decade of deftly handling his business, he ambitiously branched out to include the linen for gastronomical destination restaurants and the linens for hospitals. Having come from humble origins he had grown up only turning his mind toward s pragmatic thoughts. He now need not merely concentrate on the amassing of money as an indicator of success. To be able to invest in things such as art, which were abstracts, had become a burgeoning ambition. His wife who was of a similar back ground as he thought it slightly odd. For him it was a way to feed his soul that did not have the absolutes placed on it in the way that collecting wine did, which was a drab equation of X amount of Euros per bottle. One saved the bottle or showed it off to company then drank it. After the purchase, there was a muted pleasure that dulled more with every year as the cellar further filled and it became forgotten. Drinking it was not much better as it was a momentary fleeting pleasure with even the best vintage being put at risk if the cook used too much garlic or one had a cold. Yes, a painting upon initial purchase had an amount attached to it but there was no limit in what and how often from then on the owner could get something out of it.

He had the heaviest eyelids I had ever seen, they were like two thick wedges of blood orange, the rinds from which the fruit was scooped out then laid on their sides some distance above each cheek. He preferred drawings, executed in any medium, over paintings. His reason for this was that drawings tended to lean more towards the figurative, there was rarely the abstractions as can be found in painting. Upon initially deciding to collect art he went to museums, read some books and then visited galleries incognito. Despite the high praise some pieces received, to him there was a stylistic *the emperor has no clothes* effect. Michael did not mind putting in the work to develop his eye and at first, he worried that there may be more to the melting globs of paint and squat color fields than he realized. Then he thought of the salons at the Louvre and d'Orangerie that he had repeatedly made his way slowly through. He could see a line of descendance from one generation of artists to the next in their drawings. Some of the pieces seemed mere preparatory pieces for paintings, their place in the museum secured only on account of the artist's name but others seemed tiny worlds unto themselves. It pointed him in a direction that he wanted to go, made more appealing for not containing the inherent fear of being tricked into a painterly fad by a gallerist.

I had a small red leather folio with me in which were examples of drawings done using different mediums. It was not to expedite a sale so much as to give him something to chew over. I had already decided that I would do fresh pieces for him in whatever he fancied: graphite, ink, washes. This was flattering to him and it helped subtly underscore the fact that of course I would not mind a sale but I did not need to make one. I usually let Mai handle all this business stuff but I had been intrigued by his desire to collect strictly drawings. Often my drawings sold but usually as a sort of side deal to a painting or as a form of wall appetizer during a show.

"What do you think Michael?"

In friendship, I rarely used anyone's name unless cross with them, in business it was a strategic forced intimacy not without effect. He was going to go with six pieces, three ink and three wash pencil ones. I was getting ready to leave. There was a near compulsion on his part to further articulate his preference for drawings. His brows knitted together but the words would not come, his left hand slowly moved back and forth gripping for the unseen. I was not without patience but worried in his mind he would start to associate this new frustration with me or my work.

"It is like jazz, to hear a pianist solo, playing his songs; it is them, their power concentrated."

This seemed to him if not an exact then a good enough analogy. As he nodded relief came into his demeanor. We shook hands and I left.

I went to the market. My plan was to get everything that I would need as to be able to throw myself into my work without having to interrupt the flow once I got started with the mundane practical considerations of everyday life. I am sure it was junk science but just as I felt that the cobblestones of the Mouffe heated by the summer sun softened the tread of one's shoes to hold them there longer, in these colder months they were slicker in a not quite iced way as to push everything away and get back to the warmer months quicker. The muted colors of the root vegetables piled up on the tables which had formerly served as the base for pyramids of lemons and oranges gave an extra depth to the whisks of the herb's greens.

I would do wash pieces, still lifes of bushels of herbs. The contrasts of parsley green and that of sage already appearing in my mind's eye. For the ink pieces, I would do some nudes. Women brought out the poetry in me and between the two small series a fuller picture of my artistic identify would emerge as I was conscious of not wanting to ever be defined solely by one type of subject matter.

There was no deadline but I did not want to take too long. I was lucky in that I worked fast, for me the harder part was sometimes the subject matter. Working on the wash pieces first, the subject and compositions for which were already largely done in my head I could wait for inspiration to come for the ink pieces. Worst case scenario, I knew models, although I always preferred the spontaneous truth of a moment deriving from a more informal setting.

She had been a trapeze artist for a wreck of a circus that played the provinces of Russia and Poland. There had been an accident and she hurt herself. How it happened depended upon her mood; drunk on cheap vodka and self-loathing, then with a scowl she would say under her breath that she had missed her mark. At other times, it was the fault of fate by way of all the secondhand equipment her circus had bought to save money.

One time as we passed a pawn shop I saw a pair of ox blood wingtips in the window. As I was going to go in to see what size they were and how much they cost she caught my arm;

"No, it is bad luck to wear another man's shoes. You will take on all of their problems on top of your own."

The harness and lines that her circus had bought cheap from defunct shows had possessed the same kind of bad hoodoo.

She liked to live in cheap tenements as the halls had intermittent lighting. Kids breaking the hall lighting fixtures for bored sport, leaving just enough so that they could find their way. In this faulty light, after a few drinks if she thought no one was around then with squinted eyes she would run down the hall with a tilted back head and arms straight out, hands gripping for something that was not there.

Now by happenstance made more fortuitous by the fact that she normally did not get out of bed until late afternoon, Dina stood before me. She would make for the perfect model. Her moods were mercurial and her face, in an act of protean sympathy kept pace. Taller than me and with long limbs there was something both harsh and feminine about her, the more emphasized aspect depending upon how she was dressed. Like a lot of athletes who cease to be active her body had kept its leanness except for a little pot belly and with overindulging, a little meat under the chin.

I said hello. We went for a drink and gossiped a little. When asked what I was working on I took the opportunity to ask her if she would model. She was game and what reservations I had were momentarily silenced by the fact that she did not inquire about money. I did not want her to merely show up at the studio and position herself on a dais. We would hang out for a day or two so that I could watch her, absorb her natural body language which for most people was different than what occurred when posing. The grocery bags on the ground by my feet, the celery rested its head against my leg. I needed to get home and put everything away but before I could take my leave she beat me to it, looking at her watch and telling me that she had to go. She would come by my studio tomorrow towards the end of the day. Getting up she kissed me on the cheek, turning around after only a few steps;

"Do you want it shaved?"

"No, leave it for now."

For three days it had been slightly warmer but misty as if nature were feeling nostalgic for her springful youth. Everything accorded itself to this happy reprieve from winter with sympathy; my mood, health and the ease of starting work all going well. We went to the cafes ostensibly to chat and drink but I started doing sketches from the get-go. Her body language, she always kept herself at angles which leant themselves to an organic drama. I would be able to start on the ink pieces sooner than I thought but would still not rush. I had learned to go slower, I could finish pieces relatively quick the harder thing was to hold myself back from doing so as to see what else could come. Once I was finished with a piece I could not go back to it and tweak it should further ideas arise. By making myself slow down I allowed for more ideas to present themselves before it was too late.

I had her start to undress, she was in a white camisole which had probably been expensive but was now revealing all the nights it had seen via a series of off colored stains and patches of wear showing like scars upon the otherwise smooth silk surface. Her breasts were small and somewhat upturned. Her underwear was faded and had one bow on the left hip the other long ago having fallen off. They were too small for her and I felt that with the way they cut into her that they broke up the lines of her lower body. For half a second she let them hang off of her big toe before flinging them across the room with a kick. I had her sit at the end of the cot with her elbows on her knees. I did a quick sketch in graphite to nail down compositional lines. I got it exact but with her long frame, even sloping it made the horizontal line of the end of the bed over which her legs were draped look too small as if I had made a mistake in the proportions. I did not ever try to hide the fact that I worked at my craft but despite everything else in the sketch being good I would not give this sketch to her as to have it out there in the world, it could be misconstrued as a legitimate child of mine. I had her move over to the left side of the cot, positioning herself in the middle, feet on the floor as if about to get up. It looked much better, the cheap mattress causing her to sink down while simultaneously rising up on either side of her, a lanky giantess resting in the cream colored palm of someone even bigger. I had her place her elbows one on each knee and position her feet in a pigeon toed "V".

I was able to execute in rapid succession a series of graphite pieces slightly altering her pose as to find the most naturally emotional. As I was focusing on position of her limbs and angle of her head the bed was reduced down to guidelines which hinted at where it would be where it to totally appear in the piece. As long as she did not move much I was fine to chat.

"What kind of women do you prefer?"

I thought about my answer but forgot to say as my hand surfed the flow appearing on the paper. A few hours of sketching and I felt confident that I had found the best position. I would be able to now do the first ink piece. I captured the pose I wanted in a sketch so that I could do a piece based off of the sketch or have her once again sit using the sketch as an exacting placement guide. Having these two viable options, I could also go onto finding the next pose to sketch.

As I took a moment to mull over how I wanted to do it she told me that she was hungry. The way she said it with a laconic slowness that combined a degree of shyness with appetite accompanied by a smile like smoke which she exuded from the tiny hole above a jutted-out bottom lip. She wanted to have some of my spaghetti which she had heard about from God knows who.

"I can't eat Spaghetti for lunch, it's too filling."

"So?"

"I need to still be able to get things done."

She thought the whole thing hilarious and as she laughed her breasts fluttered in rhythm to her guffaws and from under her veil of loosened hair small pearls of teeth were in evidence.

"If you want I will make you some but I am not having any."

Dina was fine with this. Although I did not do this often with people, I brought her to my place hoping that my casualness in doing so would make her categorize the information in her head with the same importance as knowing that I rarely ate red meat and so therefore would not seem valuable enough to share. I put some Albert Ammons on and opened the wine I would need to make the sauce. She took a glass and settled on the couch. One of my sketchbooks was on the coffee table. As I reached for the mesh basket of onions atop the refrigerator she carefully flipped through the book.

"These works, they are your halo. You will be forgiven everything at some point. For your sake, hopefully sooner than later."

Only Russians had such poetic ways of asking to be fucked despite the potential consequences. The sauce was ready, it smelled so good that I decided I would have some too, tempering my portion as to not be knocked out cold.

Dina went to sit at the table but I told her the couch was fine. I poured us some more wine and put the bowls down on the coffee table. There were long tendrils of fragrant steam rising up from the bowls so I knew there must be a wait. I put on the other side of the record. She was resting her bowl on the shelf of her stomach which was protruding more than usual only because she was leaning back into the embrace of the couch. She blew on the fork whose middle was fattened by the pasta entwined upon it. Some of the sauce hit her chin. It caused her to look down at her blouse with a worry that abated as soon as she saw no sauce had splattered there too.

I went into the kitchen to get her a dishtowel to tuck into her shirt. I stood in the doorway watching her. Eating with gusto, Dina was not allowing it to cool but instead opted to take a big swallow of wine between each bite, swirling it around in her mouth hoping that it would not only cool but coat. Her cheeks were flushed and her forehead dotted with beads of perspiration. There was an erotic earthiness to it made all the more powerful by the organic way in which it had appeared. She looked up, antennae of spaghetti whipping about until blowing kiss puckered lips retracted them in.

I handed her the towel and sat back down next to her joining in but blowing on my fork first. The scent of the food and wine with an undernote of her musk was an olfactory prompt. One of the pieces would be the scene unfolding before me with only some minor compositional choreography.

The front door had been painted a heavy white by the previous tenant. It wore a sash of sunlight across its top panel. I put a pillow from the couch down as I knew from personal experience the floor could be hard. I had her sit on the floor framed by the rectangle of the door. Her shirt came off but I gave her the towel and bowl of pasta back. The pillow kept putting a slight rise under her, the only way to prevent this was for her to create a pressure that there was no way for her to maintain indefinitely and whose discomfort defeated the purpose of the pillow. She tossed the pillow back on the couch as I placed my chair a few feet back, across from her. I asked her to not raise her head past a certain point but other than that she had a certain freedom of movement, as much as one would need while eating.

With her legs crossed, head slightly bowed she resumed eating. In this position her belly was more prominent with a smiley face crease appearing in the region slightly above her naval. The heat of the meal and her general enjoyment mixed with the wine collaborating to write a poem of pleasure upon her body in dark pinks and flushed reds. Before she draped the two top corners of the towel over her shoulders I noticed that her areoles, a dark purple with the nipples, two small rosebuds.

I was able to execute a sketch in graphite which was spot on. I do not know if it was just in my head but when I looked at the towel, it seemed as if it had been added to cover up a mistake or weak spot, its mass even with the effect of depth from creases became a compositional dead spot. I asked Dina to remove the towel. I crumpled it into a ball with one corner extended short tail like and placed it diagonally from her left knee on the floor. In work, I felt freer to really study her body and not have it be misconstrued. There was a fine downy line of hair that went from her naval down to her sex, which like her breasts was a pert upturned mound collared by hair and the shadow of indentations at the furthest point of each side where leg met body.

I did not tear up the towel version as it was still good and my feeling on the effect of the towel could change tomorrow as it sometimes did with a drawing that was not an outright misfire. I got up to get a pen which I had filled with a viscous red ink some time ago, hoping that inactivity had not dried it out.

I had to run the tip of the pen under the tap but otherwise it was not too gummed up, with the ink flowing smoothly. I heard the clatter of her fork hitting the side of the bowl and so brought the bottle of wine with me. She had used the time to stretch out her limbs, leaning her head back making it rotate from left to right while simultaneously rolling her shoulders. Grabbing her glass off the coffee table, I poured her some wine. The bowl was empty, abstract expressionist smear of red ring marking the tide line of where the sauce had been. I took the bowl and placed it opposite the napkin, handing her the wine. I asked her if she could hold the leaned back position supported by her left arm in a semi turn, palm planted flat on the floor one hip pointed towards the ceiling with her knees together. I got the angle I wanted, the look of one possibly about to lay on their side in an unfurled fetal position. The napkin and empty bowl while good devices to allow me to show off my chops made the composition look too much the academic still life, so I removed them.

She drank slowly, always returning her arm to the same position after each sip. I wanted to do some detailed studies of her eyes and face as to be able to do some other pieces with emotional authenticity at a later date. Distracted I had forgotten to open a window which combined with the food and being naked for so long made her face become flushed, her eyes limpid. I dipped my finger into her glass which was now empty except for a few drops and some flake like sediment. I painted her lips with it. I filled up several pages with noses, lips and eyes as seen at different angles.

I wanted coffee but there were too many dishes from our meal to contend with.

"That should be enough for today, let's go grab a coffee."

I would have to assess all that I did but I knew for sure that at least one of my pieces was basically ready to be framed and I had more than enough studies to do other pieces from were that the only one. I brought the dishes into the kitchen to soak in the sink as she got dressed.

I asked her if she minded walking a little. After having been still for so long she was more than glad to. I headed us towards Port Royal. As I did so often when walking with someone else, as we passed one of the many historical plaques which adorned so many of the cities buildings, I pointed it out. Dina did not stop but gave it a quick look in case she had misheard me and it was something more than the dates proclaiming when Victor Hugo had lived there. Having slowed down but not stopped we were now well past the plaque, she had not said anything but merely gave a gentle shrug which could have almost passed for adjusting her pocketbook's strap.

We took a seat at a café on the side of the street in the sun. I almost felt like a drink but the coffee craving won out. Dina had similar thoughts but said "the same" to the doe eyed waitress who seemed taken by her, spending time after delivering our coffees pretending to fold napkins at the waiters' station to observe us and see if we were together. The coffee was good and strong, I let each sip linger on my tongue, it was the simple pleasures which were the treasures that made me rich. We sat in silence and as I had given her the chance to talk but she had not needed to, I took out my small sketch-pad.

"So you do not like Victor Hugo?" I asked.

Like a lot of people she had to read him in school, the Tale of Two Cities being given a sort of pro-communist slant in its interpretation. I liked Victor Hugo, despite some pot boiler tendencies but it was not just that specific plaque which excited me. Working in Paris I felt a connection to my artistic forefathers and heroes as I did things my way but walked the same streets whose ambient light had changed very little if at all since their time.

I started to explain this to Dina as I did not want her to think my little charge had been exclusively a Victor Hugo thing. She understood what I was getting at and was respectful of my philosophy but clearly did not share it. What had brought her here? Her eyes grew distant but mercenary as if trying to recall the price of something sold long ago. For her, Paris had always been a shorthand for plenty of good things to eat. Plenty to eat and no lines to wait in to get it. All one needed was money and even fools could come by that. She was not immune to the galleries and museums but the appeal to her had always been more pragmatic. She also figured that upon initially moving here if she became someone's mistress she would not be cloistered away in some dacha along with other prized possessions and could carve out a life for herself during her down time.

I did not need her to come back with me as I wanted to do variations on her eyes and lips, building up a sort of muscle memory which would allow me to make her lines appear anytime easily at will, leaving me to concentrate on the emotional aspect. She was going to catch the metro and I walked a ways with her to the station.

We passed another plaque which was for a general, the military ones holding no interest for me, prompting her to smile and ask me;

"How long will you stay here?"

She eventually wanted to move someplace warm and by the sea. I liked the ocean too but if I had to choose between the two then the concrete always won out. We kissed goodbye, I watched her descend the stairs.

Now alone with my thoughts, I wondered if I could ever leave. No, it was too important to my work, the city itself always serving as a sort of battery. By way of giving thanks I turned around and decided to walk a little, heading down Boulevard Montparnasse. I decided to have a drink, I pretend that it is a random left I take onto Rue du Montparnasse and stop at Falstaff's, far from my usual type of haunt. It was all dark wood and open secrets and one would feel as if they had stepped into a scene from someone else's movie were there just a touch more merriment or melancholy. They emphasized beer and so to stay in the spirit of the place I cheated on my Pastis with a Belgian. I made effort to file away the ambient light for some future piece. I would come back again but I was not sure when as there were so many places to drink and sketch and only so many hours in the day, days in the week. After chatting but not flirting with the waitress I enjoyed giving the extra surprise of a large tip which she would not discover until after I was gone as I did not know her unlike my regular places I did not feel the need to wait to say goodbye to her before departing.

I had enjoyed my beer but was now reminded why I preferred the harder stuff as a full feeling hit me. I decided to continue walking, heading further down Rue Montparnasse. I once again mused on Paris and my place within the city.

In literature, there were always all the coincidences, the potboiler devices of Dickens and Hugo. For myself, I sought instead connections which were organic and there to find in real life if one is observant enough. All the artists of every era, seemingly different but upon closer examination, more akin to links in a chain. Each generation encompasses a diverse array of artists of whom it would not necessarily appear that they have commonalities in their styles or goals but are still united in how their struggles and new conceptualization free up the next era's artists.

Painter Theodore Gericault (1791-1824) started out with a formal education which provided him with the typical classical foundation. He was mercurial in mood but talented which allowed him to foster the support of some of his teachers even as he chafed more and more under the traditional system of study. Gericault felt that neoclassicism was a pretty but bloated thing, lacking natural tension and release. Increasingly he felt that even the better contemporary works being created in this style were stillborn. He left his formal studies to pursue his own education copying and studying the great works at The Louvre (1810-1812) which stopped when he was banned from the museum for roughing up a fellow student.

The Charging Chasseur (1812) was his first work to garner notice and a burgeoning fame for the painter. It rejected the established classical composition template and also shows a (then) contemporary event. This first triumph was followed by *Wounded Cuirassier Leaving the Battle* (1814) which was controversial among critics when it was shown at that year's salon. It served as a companion piece to the previous painting but was done using a palette of somber colors as was often found in the palette of the northern painters whom he admired such as Peter Paul Rubens (1577-1640) and Rembrandt Harmenszoon van Rijn (1606-1669). It also showed pain and encroaching death not as a necessarily noble, abstract thing. This would later be an often utilized component in Delacroix's works. The mixed reception of his work offended his ego causing Gericault to take a self-imposed exile.

As was the common practice for individuals who had the means, Gericault had initially bought a substitute for his required military service which was a person given money to do another's term of conscription (1811-1814). He now went to serve in the mounted Second Squadron of the Paris National Guard, then the First Company of Musketeers of the King. His regiment was to follow the king into exile but was disbanded en-route. Due to Napoleon's proclamation about Royal military personal in not being allowed in Paris during this time Gericault kept a low profile. With the king's return to the throne (July 1815) Gericault's term of service was over and he resumed his Parisian life, mixing socially with artists, thinkers and career military who helped facilitate his access to the stables in Versailles where he was allowed to further study equestrian anatomy.

In 1816 Gericault made a try for the Prix De Rome. This was a scholarship award created in 1663 by Louis XIV. It was for painters, sculptures and composers with other fields slowly being added over time. Artist were expected to submit a work specifically for the competition and upon winning were to have a residency of three to five years at the Palazzo Mancini. In 1803 Napoleon Bonaparte moved the prize winner's residency to The Villa Medici. While serving their residency the winners were expected to create a work. From the time, the residency was moved to the Villa Medici the list of those who won and now great artists who did not place reads like a who's who of artistic immortals. Many of the winners who would go on to great fame such as Hector Berlioz (won 1830) and Claude Debussy (1884) did not like life at the villa, stretching the attendance rules to the limit.

In 1816 Gericault tried but failed to win the prize. He decided to go to Italy anyways. Gericault traveled to Italy (Florence, Rome and Naples) where he studied the Renaissance masters finding particular inspiration from Titian and Michelangelo. He planned to do a massively sized frieze which looked to the artistic past in its format but portrayed the still existent rider less horse race down The Corso in all its unadulterated emotion which closed out every carnival. Gericault never undertook the work, only going as far as making a series of preparatory sketches before going back to France.

The next two years were spent working on the painting which would become known as *The Raft of Medusa*. It was a contemporary event which was still politically controversial which was why he submitted it to the salon of 1819 as *A Shipwreck Scene*.

The Medusa was a ship government frigate which was part of a convoy bringing soldiers and emigrates to Senegal. Due to navigational error on the part of the captain the ship ran aground in the shallows off of the West African Coast. The captain was not able to refloat the boat, largely because he refused to eject the ship's 24 pounder guns, so after a few days the ship began breaking up.

In general, the ship was ill equipped for a massive at sea exodus. The captain and officers took the strongest of the life boats of which there were way too few to accommodate all. A raft was improvised for all those who could not get onto a boat made from planks and rope. The Captain promised to tow the raft but for one reason or another the tow cable got lost.

One hundred and fifty people had to squeeze onto a raft measuring 24 meters by 7. In the panic and confusion they were given no charts, oars rudders or even a semblance of a leader. Three days into being adrift hallucinations and delirium along with acts of cannibalism occurred among the tiny raft's population. By the seventh day there were only twenty-seven people left, thirteen of whom were either sick or insane. What little food there was to eat were mainly the flying fish caught off the raft's side. It was difficult to divide up so it was decided to execute the dying rather than waste what little resources remained.

After six more days fifteen people remained alive. A ship was seen off in the distance but the raft was riding too low in the water and despite their cries they went unnoticed, their brief exaltation turning to a soul crushing melancholy. Later in the day the ship, called Then Argus, doubled back and found the raft. Upon rescue five of the raft's occupants died almost immediately. There would be only ten survivors pulled from the sea one of which was the ship's surgeon Henri Savigny.

Henri would file an official report on the entire episode omitting nothing. The newly restored King would take a lot of blame for the incident in the public court of opinion. While he had not been involved directly in the assigning of the captain, the part of the governmental cabinet that had was always strongly a royalist institution. Henri wanted the guilty to be punished and for all the families of those who died to receive the proper compensation. His report was viewed as a black eye for the royalist government. The fact that the navy tribunal only gave the captain a light slap on the wrist shows that they had already made their minds up to bury the report. With some foresight, probably on the part of Henri, the report was leaked to the press, first appearing in *Journal des Debats* and fairly soon after that being translated into English for *The Times*. The government made no move to compensate nor even hint at contrition. Henri and another survivor, naval engineer Alexandre Corréard wrote a book detailing the ordeal of those on the raft. The Captain officially was none the worse for the incident whereas Alexandre and Henri were dismissed from the governmental posts. The book sold well in England and France but the two authors would find themselves relentlessly harassed and persecuted. With the popularity of the book and the entire debacle becoming public knowledge the government made an amazingly bad attempt at a cover up too far after the fact. The way the government had handled it, with their initial wrong doing, persecution of the victim(s) and mistakes compounded by sloppy attempts at cover-up would occur again a generation later with The Dreyfus Affair (1894-1906).

Gericault wanted fame and all its accompanying accoutrements but on his own terms. Loosely stated, part of his artistic philosophy was in mixing the events of his times while utilizing the dramatic structures of baroque painting without lapsing into an overstuffed classicism. The story of the survivors was near on biblical in its bleak violence and would make the perfect vessel to transmit his artistic ideals.

There was much preparatory work for the piece. Gericault became friends with both Henri and Alexandre and would endlessly sketch the episodes that they told him. He would go to the ocean to make sketches and observe the mariner lighting. He interviewed some of the other survivors besides the two authors of the account. Gericault would go to hospitals as to observe the faces of patients in various phases of dying. He also borrowed a severed head from an insane asylum which he kept on the roof of his studio to observe and sketch. He got Henri and Alexandre to pose for him and had Alexandre who had built the actual raft, make another in same manner and size. Another component to the work was compositional choreography which was inspired by recollections of the Michelangelo frescoes he had seen. With this piece, he was not setting out to create a work whose chief aim was social criticism. Despite all of his exhaustive research, the painting is not accurate in regard to how the survivors on the raft would look. Absent are any signs of privation on the skin of the raft's occupants. However, that had never been an important part of his mission with this piece. As he had wanted to do with his Roman horse race painting, Gericault created a massive piece which took a current event and portrayed it rife with drama. Mixing naturalists elements with grand manner, it can be seen as if not the first then the immediate precursor to Romantic Era painting of which Eugene Delacroix is often cited as the embodiment of (a young Delacroix met Gericault in Guerin's studio where some of the Medusa work was being done and would pose as one of the raft's occupants).

Whether it was a modicum of restraint or Gericault feared that the salon committee (1819) would not accept the submission, he had thinly veiled the painting's subject matter with a generic title. As much as the government wanted to begin the process of forgetting the Medusa incident they knew that to reject the painting could very well cause a flare up of attention in the nation's conscience. Already being friends with two of the raft's survivors and chief architects behind seeking out justice, it was feared that to ignore or disrespect the massive work would only serve as a catalyst to get Gericault deeper involved in the survivor's plight. This logic aside there were an insightful few who also, while finding the piece bleak acknowledge that there was something to it.

He was awarded a medal and given a commission for a religious piece of which having little interest, he would secretly pass on to Delacroix letting him keep the fee. The state passed on buying the piece for the national collection (which they would eventually do a few years after Gericault's death). The sum total of Gericault's triumphs at the salon being the equivalent of a backhanded compliment.

The undertaking of the massive work combined with disappointment and the inherent drama which was part of his life sapped him of energy. He decided to go on tour with the painting to England whose equine culture still greatly appealed to him.

While in London he mixed with the upper crust, horse breeders and landed gentry but also went out among the poor whose plight inspired him to do a series of lithographs. His were not the first (contemporary) street scenes ever done but he did them in a completely unromanticized way. Showing nothing charming about a life on the street or the bottom rung of society. It was the start of a deeper realism in his work as the suffering of the poor and the working class was not exaggerated for drama's sake nor to get any agenda across. These works, showing every walk of society were with their visual vernacular anti-classical in style, yet powerfully dramatic as a finer degree of subtlety appeared with his leaning towards a more realism style.

During his English stay Gericault would execute works in several mediums (watercolor, oil and lithographs). It was his lithographs which seemed to have gotten him to move further away from classical trappings, even though in past works he had somewhat transmuted them from their rigidity of structure. There had always been a sort of Republican aspect towards print making and lithographs. It made art more accessible to those not on the upper tier of society and able to collect or attend salons. Part of this was that works could be shown in any bookstore or privately via a folio without having to go through the official salon/museum system then in play. To make the works was an easier accomplishment financially, with no patron nor commission needed ahead of time. As the works tended to be smaller than a painting and to some degree utilized the same technology as advertisement and entertainment event posters, on a subconscious level the powers that be often thought them less potentially subversive. Although some of the works were of jockeys and animals too, with his street scenes Gericault sought to show slices of daily life in a non-dogmatic way.

Back in France (winter 1821) he struck up a friendship with Étienne-Jean Georget (1795-1829) who was a pioneer of forensic psychiatry. He would do a series of studies based off of some of his patients. *Portraits of the Insane* (1822-23) was a series of ten portraits of people suffering from various conditions such as kleptomania, delusions of military command and obsessive envy. Of the series of ten only five have survived. They are all executed in a realistic style with no exaggerations needed to achieve drama. They show how in some ways, with technique and vision there was a cross pollination with his lithographs and desire towards a more naturalistic streak. Like lithographs the works were also meant to serve as a more accessible vehicle to get, if not an idea, then an image out there. The works were seen by Étienne as a way for other professionals and family of the sufferers of the conditions to study the afflicted without the trauma or parading the actual patients out in an undignified and possibly risky way.

Towards the end of his short life he was planning to once again do an epic piece which utilized something then current. The ideas of something to do with the then waning but still feared Spanish inquisition or an African slave market were considered. After the epic Raft piece, he had been leaning further towards the side of realism while minimizing the classical components that he had so successfully transmuted for The Raft. There is no way of knowing what the gestated piece would have looked like but most likely it would have further underscored the connection to next two successive painters who would use aspects of Gericault's pictorial vocabulary (Delacroix & Courbet). Gericault had suffered from chronic ill health which included tuberculosis. A series of horseback riding accidents had further exasperated his already fragile health. There was also in all probability an aspect of spiritual fatigue involved in his decline too as he spent his life honing an individualized voice which he refused to compromise while also wanting to achieve fame. A goal made harder by the system which he had to utilize and that was hostile to any sort of stylistic changes. Despite this struggle, his fingertips had kept brushing the gold ring just often enough to spur him on in his struggle until the end. A similar thing would occur in varying degrees too for both Delacroix and Courbet.

Shortly after the time of his death, depending upon your point of view, the final slight or a last great honor occurred. Comte de Forbin, curator for the Louvre secured purchase by the state for *The Raft of Medusa* where it can still be seen today.

While in the midst of doing all his work on *The Raft of Medusa*, Gericault still occasionally used former teacher Guerin's studios. A young Delacroix was able to see the work as it unfolded, even posing as one of the raft's survivors. It excited him to create his first large work *Dante and Virgil in Infernal Regions* for the salon of 1822. Compositionally, it harkens back to Gericault's raft and choreography of the renaissance painters. Subject wise, it was safe, conveying an episode from Dante's *Inferno* which was still in line with the expected mission of painters which was to have their works serve a social or moral purpose via biblical or other moral subject matter. Even with remaining in line with the approved subject matter, his painting which he wanted to show at the salon of 1822 was considered radical on account of his chosen palette and brushstroke technique. The salon committee and public would largely be against the work. One of the exceptions was jury member Antonie-Jean Gros (1771-1835). Gros found the painting different but good, taking it under his wing and having his personal framer frame it while seeing too that it was properly hung. Gros for most of his career painted in the neoclassical style and often like Jacque Louis David (1748-1825) whom he studied under, his works served a socio-political purpose.

Eugene Delacroix (1798- 1863) is often called the father of Romantic painting, he built off of aspects of what Gericault had done. Combining some of the same components but in different degrees than his predecessor while also mixing in other influences and his own innate talent. With his works he often brought forth the worship/idealization of Byronic, fatalistic beauty so much a tenant of romantic era art in all mediums. There were also more often present less outwardly transmuted components of neoclassicism elements combined with those which we think of now as quintessential romantic ones as exemplified by *The Apotheosis of Napoleon* and *Liberty Leading the People* which seems more the spiritual child of David or Gros than Gericault.

His contemporary, Ingres once referred to Delacroix as a "Drunken broom" for his use of colors for effect over finer detail work. This technique would carry over as part of the base foundation of the next generation of painters, the impressionists. From 1839 to 1857 Delacroix would try for a seat on The Academie de Beaux Arts. On his seventh try at the age of fifty-nine he would finally succeed. The older Delacroix would champion the burgeoning impressionists Edouard Manet (1832-1883). Sick with the tuberculosis which would eventually contribute to his death, he made it a point to go to see Manet's painting at Galerie Martinet. He would vote for Manet's *The Absinthe Drinker* to show in the salon of 1863 after having his academie chair for a mere two years. Throughout his life Delacroix would receive official accolades, begrudgingly and usually far after the fact. Throughout his career his work followed the pattern of inspiring other artists while publicly garnering both fame and revulsion.

For his entire life, Delacroix was inspired by literature. Interacting with some of the brightest literary lights of his era while also being well versed in classical and European literature. He had less a republican motive in his print and etching work than Gericault, combining his love of literature with his raison d'être, he lent his work to many books including works by Shakespeare, Walter Scott and Johann Wolfgang von Goethe. Delacroix spent his entire life working in several visual mediums. Combing a precision with emotional complexity, his print making did not show any type of radical departure from what had come before him. Neither was there a mission to use a medium which allowed for the less privileged to be able to have access to art. Delacroix's lithographs especially as could be found in books were done for his own pleasure and the lifelong deep affection he felt for literature.

Each generation's artistic vanguard faces the struggle to free themselves from the established ways of doing or thinking. While their battles do not necessarily result in wholesale wins via eventual acceptance, they do provide direction for the following generations of artists by giving them things to build off of, incorporate or equally as important, avenues not to pursue.

Delacroix could be seen as an unofficial figurehead of an era's painters and while he, like Gericault before, him had some of what they did directly absorbed into the next generation of artists, there was never a formalized *school of* for either painter. Gericault and Delacroix had issues with the salon system although neither was ever able to make a wholesale break from it. Both painters had sought to find new templates to replace the stagnating neoclassicism which was then the accepted foundation for all painters. As both painters continued to find certain renaissance masters an inspiration and also still had to operate within a system which would not reward too radical of a departure, the neoclassicism would not completely be eradicated from their works by their brushes but instead would be buried under components which would help to contribute to burgeoning romanticism and later supply fertile soil from which would spring realism and impressionism. For both painters too, there was never an overall specific amount of each device, whether it be the realism precursor touches or emotional romantic colorations that stayed the same from work to work. Some of their works leaned further towards what had come before them while others offered a visual foreshadowing of what their efforts would go on to inspire.

The painters Gustave Courbet (1819-77), Jean Francois Millet (1814-75) and Honoré Daumier (1808-79) each went even further than Gericault and Delacroix in their rejection of neoclassicism. Although they did not work together as a formalized group each of these three painters greatly contributed to birthing the genre of naturalist painting. Before these painters there had been aspects of what they would fully utilize dating all the way back to the deglamorized blood and sweat biblical scene paintings of Caravaggio (1571-1610). From within this genre would be aspects used to create genres such as the Barbizon school, naturalists and further ingredients which would go towards impressionism and the symbolists.

Courbet would show everyday people living their lives with a realistic psychological complexity and not merely the one-dimensional emotional cadence as occurred in mythology and parables used to push the narrative theme of a work forth.

His *A Burial at Orans* (1849-50) is a good example of his overall artistic mission. The work shows the recent funeral of his uncle which he had attended. The work's size, 10x22 feet was of a size was of symbolic importance as larger pieces were usually used for conveying important religious or socio-political events. All the subjects in the work where those who had been there and not professional models, a method which would later often be used by the impressionists. At the actual funereal, lacking is the expected overall feeling of a state of grace being achieved by the deceased or those attending the burial. Instead the viewer as voyeur is privy to the diversity of emotions as actually occur at such events, from boredom to distraction, dour stoicism to a sort of somewhat reluctantly just going through the motions as others are watching. There is a dog front and center gently mocking perhaps all the saccharine death bed genre works where the departing is surrounded under glowing candle light by a coterie of friends and family including the family dog. The presence of the dog in so prominent a place in this piece also serves to add a rustic touch further reminding the viewer that it is no high upper-class tableau as a work of this size was often in the service of.

Courbet would early in his career try lithography but to no great results. His main medium would remain the brush and canvas. Despite some official recognition Courbet sought an end or at least an alternative to the salon system. When his works including "Burial.." was rejected by the important Exposition Universelle (1865) out of his own pocket he created an alternative by erecting a temporary show right next to the official one titled "The Pavilion of Realism". Both Delacroix and Baudelaire supported this effort but most of the general public who attended did so out of mere curiosity or to mock it. His use of everyday people living their lives and rejection of gallery hierarchy would be a direct inspiration to the up and coming impressionists and naturalists, who were like the realist but with an even more raw reportage (without any kind of message/agenda) bent to their work.

His political activism would manifest itself in a more dogmatic form as a friendship with theorists/activist Pierre Joseph Proudhon (1809-65) spurred him into the political arena for which he was ill equipped. The good to come of this was that during the rise of The Paris Commune (1871) he was made in charge of all of the cities museums and instead of mere posturing and speech making, managed to save many important works of art from looters or those merely looking for some sort of payback via breaking things. While he diligently executed this task, the revolution lost steam, fractured and then amidst meetings of committees and subcommittees imploded. Even with the initial sincere revolutionary zeal many of those who had steered the uprising proved more adept at saving their own hides than they had in maintaining the new order. Courbet was left out in the cold, unprotected. On paper he had more power to get things aside from art conservation done than was probably the truth. The restored provisional government fined Courbet and he spent several months in jail. Rather than risk potentially facing further hostility of the new provisional government he went into self-imposed exile in Switzerland. What things he had not brought with him into exile were seized by the state and his friends and family harassed by a constant state sponsored surveillance. He was found guilty and held responsible for paying 323,091 francs to restore the Vendome Column. The dismantling of The Vendome Column which during the days of the commune supposedly occurred from a suggestion which he had made but which had actually been made before he was named to his office, Courbet only suggesting in a written petition a more respectful dismantling and moving of it. In a show or mercy, he would be allowed to make yearly payments the fine being paid in full falling somewhere around his 91st birthday. Before the first payment was due, Courbet would pass away due to liver complications after a lifetime of heavy drinking which had increased while in exile.

Honoré Daumier (1808-79) was a painter and lithographer. His father and grandfather before him had been glaziers which was a job that combined selling and making frames with painting passe-partout pictures, in Marseilles. When Honoré was only seven his father quit his job to go to Paris and try his hand at being a poet. He was presented to King Louis

XVIII and enjoyed a brief two weeks of fame. There is no particular thing which caused him to fall by the wayside. There was the fact that he had no real "in" with Parisian society and that he was most likely looked upon during the period of his fame as a mere amusement or novelty of the moment. His failure was made worse by having so briefly tasted success and he would have a nervous breakdown which would affect the trajectory of Honoré's early life.

From an early age Honoré showed an interest in drawing which his family did not initially support. While in his early teens, his father's incapacity served as catalyst for him to seek a way to earn money. First he served as a go-to for a bailiff which would introduce him to the many types of court workers he would later go on to caricature. From that job, he found himself working for a bookseller in the arcades of the Palais-Royal which was then one of the busiest spots in all of Paris, attracting people from every strata of Parisian society. While he did a brief turn apprenticing under family friend and art conservationist Alexander Lenoir (1822) he was able to study his collection of baroque art and the Rubens in his personal collection.

To earn money he would do prints and lithographs often in a generic, workman like style and usually of the celebrities of the day which he would leave unsigned or signed by Zéphirin Belliard who he apprenticed under and who was already known for his lithograph portraits. One of his first original caricature works was sold in 1822 when he was only fifteen. This served to steel his resolve to make a go at the life of an artist but with the pragmatic plan of earning his living with something connected to his brush and pen.

In 1830's the censorship laws post July Revolution are relaxed and Daumier becomes a staff member for *La Caricature*. He lampoons King Louis-Philippe likening him to the Rabelais character Gargantua. The first satirical barbs were taken if not good naturedly by the King then silently. Daumier's second attack which the King felt unprovoked raised his ire. He and the publishers were fined 500 francs each and given six months in jail with Daumier being the only one who had to actually serve time, two in a state prison and four in a mental hospital. The journal was seized putting the staff out of work and all the remaining lithographs were seized and the lithographic stone destroyed.

Upon release Daumier worked on small clay busts of the people he would caricature, as to be able to give his pieces greater depth; using the busts in lieu of them posing. The busts were put in the window of his publisher when not in use to serve as a sort of advertisement. Most of them were of the royalist supporters and upper echelons of society. At first glance, they look very much like the official busts meant to honor which could be found in public buildings around the city. It was only at closer inspection satirical flourishes could be noticed. Included in his sculptural coterie was one bust of Louis-Philippe which he kept hidden. In 1835 the September Law made illegal all political caricature. This policy would be upheld until the revolution of 1848.

Although he counted some sculptors among his friends, Daumier for the most part socialized with the regular working-class inhabitants of his neighborhood. He would go to the cafes not to talk shop with his artistic peers as was the usual practice but to people watch with his worker neighbors. Usually he also avoided attending salons or making the expected studio visits to his peers, preferring instead to drink cheap red wine with workers in dark little bars. Daumier would avoid legal trouble by now switching his focus to social commentary on the upper-class mores of the men of finance and law. He often framed his social satire within the adventures of a character, Robert Macaire.

Daumier's politics leaned heavily to the left, counting among his friends some radical liberals. He hoped for and believed far sweeping changes were needed which would make educational and living opportunities better for the poor. A factor which he felt held things back was the greed of those on the top rungs of society. In the early 1840's he aimed his satirical barbs at lawyers with his series of forty lithographs *Les Gens de Justice*.

Charles Baudelaire (1821-67) aside from being an important poet, was a perceptive essayist typically writing about other artists who were great but misunderstood or ignored by the general public (Delacroix, Manet et al) He and Daumier first struck up a friendship in 1845. The only serious article to be written about Daumier during his lifetime was by Baudelaire (May 1857) which began with:

"Nous ne connaissons, à Paris, que deux hommes qui dessinent aussi bien que M. Delacroix, l'un d'une manière analogue, l'autre dans une méthode cont raire.—L'un est M. Daumier, le caricaturiste; l'autre, M. Ingres, le grand peintre, l'adorateur rusé de Raphael. (We only know two men in Paris who draw as well as Mr. Delacroix; one using the same method as him and the other a contrary one. They are Mr. Daumier, the cartoonist and Mr. Ingres, the great painter, worshipper of Raphael)."

During the revolution of 1848 (Feb) Louis Philippe was deposed and political censorship in the press was lightened. Daumier did a series of political commentary lithographs and attended a meeting to put into play non-juried salon shows which Delacroix also attended. By way of trying to generate positive propaganda the newly elected Republic government holds a competition for painters to come up with a new image for the Republic. Courbet talked Daumier into submitting an image and he was one of the twenty finalists who received 500 francs to finish his work. Taking advantage of the freedom of the press, Daumier continued on with his political caricatures too.

By December Louis Napoleon was elected President of the Republic. Freedom of the press was systematically tightened. Much to his regret, Daumier had never able to just be a painter but continued making commercial lithographs and contributing to the journals. He began working on painting more and in 1853 made what would become annual summer pilgrimages to Almondois and Barbizon. Millet also spent time there painting and the two struck up a friendship. Daumier's draftsmanship in drawing and lithography will be an admitted influence on the figurative aspects of Millet's work.

The pastoral setting with its luminescent ambience served as a catalyst for the realists and naturalist painters. Daumier started to utilize light effect components that would be one of the recognizable marked traits of the impressionists. He would have mutual admiration for two of that movement's chief progenitors Manet (1832-83) and Monet (1840-1926).

Daumier is sometimes referred to as the first impressionist. He clearly was applying some techniques that would later be a basic part of the movement's structure but his was not the sole influence and there was never a direct mirroring of what he had done. Both he and they would be interested in the emotional potential of light and how its luminescence as observed in real life could bring forth new qualities in painting. As he delved deeper into this new form of painting he began to do artistic lithographs which were not satirical but also done in the impressionistic manner.

There was little public interest in the modern styled work by him in either medium. None of the journals which he had contributed to for decades were interested in his non-satirical work. The main one for which he had provided content, *Le Charivari*, dismissed him (1860). The cataloging of this part of his oeuvre has traditionally (pre-1938) been handled incorrectly with the numbers and dates of the works being assigned by historians of the lithographs in relation to the paintings coming first. More logically the dates and numbers should go by the lithographs as originating first, many of whose subjects and images would go on to become mirrored in paintings.

After a lithographic work which involved the constant reworking of the limestone to perfect an image it would make no sense to then wait years to execute the same theme on canvas or to painstakingly complete a canvas using such a then (unorthodox) style and wait to do a lithograph on the same theme. Daumier's own notebooks were often sparse and in his own shorthand in regard to what he worked on when which further muddied attempts at time lines. This artistic phase did not receive a lot of public attention which made contemporary accounts in other's correspondence and journals almost nonexistent.

Temporarily abandoning his radical path, In 1860 Daumier executed a woodprint *The Drunkenness of Silenus*. This is a mythological tale of a satiated satyr which Daumier still managed to subtly infuse with socio-political commentary by not deviating from the traditional classical setting but inserting the face of a Dr. Veron, publisher of the newspaper *The Constitutional* for Silenus. The composition draws upon the influence of Titian's *Triumph of Silenus* and Gericault's work of 1816 of the same name. Whether people were aware of the subtle satire or not the piece proved popular.

Despite the works popularity Daumier was having financial and health concerns. He continued on in his forward-thinking painting and lithographic work. To earn his daily bread, he still did commercial graphic work but his ambitions and passions now lay in his serious work. Even with public and critical indifference to his non-satirical output he was surrounded by a small loyal circle that tries to help him out as best they could. When he had to start selling furniture to pay bills he was given a series of small watercolor commissions. In 1863 having not turned in any work for which he had been advanced the 500 francs by The Republic, his Silenus work was seized by the state as payment.

Some of his friends and new admirers joined the editorial board of the journal *Le Charivari*, rehiring him. He continued doing his pure lithographic work and painting while also doing the more commercial prints for which he had initially been known. This was the start of a temporary upswing of both his fortune and reputation. Daumier received two commissions for train prints and one of an omnibus from an American industrialist. In 1865 *Histoire de la Caricature Moderne* was published and prominently made mention of him while also featuring a poem about him by Baudelaire. He uses this upswing to move to Valmondois.

Now living outside of Paris and with failing eyesight, he was emboldened to do some of his most political work featuring anti-imperialist and anti-Prussian Military messages. He had continued on with painting, now also utilizing the medium of watercolors. His watercolors seem slightly more accessible as they often contain episodic narratives. He entered several in the 1869 salon which garnered positive attention, the newspaper *Le Figaro* publicly demanding that Daumier be awarded the cross of the legion. Begrudgingly he would be offered it a year later but with his difference in politics he politely declined.

During the Paris Commune of 1871 he was one of artists to serve on art commission helping with museum conservation. His graphic work meant for public consumption took on an added strength but also darkness as he recorded the turbulent times with a series of governments and battles making his nation seem as if ever in a state of flux.

A year before his death he is given a solo show, facilitated by his friend Geoffroy-Dechaume at Galerie Durand-Ruel. Daumier was going through an eye operation in an attempt to fix his sight which proved to be unsuccessful and so was not able to attend. The show proved to be successful but the general consensus was that it was out of respect for his political activism more than his paintings. With a body of work that encompasses some 4000 lithographs and the same number of illustrations plus paintings done in both oil and watercolor Daumier is chiefly remembered for his satirical cartoons or as a footnote to the realists/naturalists/impressionists. From 1848 onwards though he showed himself to be a serious painter with new techniques cross pollinating not just between his graphic and painterly work but between himself and other up and coming artists as well. He did not solely influence or create a new genre but like the best artists before him contributed in numerous ways to what would come next.

Both Millet and the following group of painters who would be labeled as impressionists pulled aspects of what the artistic forbearers before them had utilized. For Millet, it was the continued and increased use of everyday people going about their lives while further rejecting neoclassicism in both subject and composition. Courbet and Daumier, with whom he had interaction, would be influential. The Barbizon area would become a "school" for those who painted there, using the scenic terrain and also to varying degrees the plein air effects of ambient light. Some of the painters who would go on to become cornerstones of the impressionist school would spend time in Barbizon. Each impressionist would bring their own brilliance to the art of painting, furthering its evolution but from the generations immediately preceding them would be the ideas of: rejecting neoclassicism in favor of regular people, fellow artists and friends as subjects, revolutionary use of color and lighting effects over cold precession and emotion over academic technique.

Millet did not really delve much into graphic work. At various times throughout their careers some of the impressionists made some prints (Pissarro, Degas et al) but it was a small part of their oeuvre taking smaller precedents than the painting, watercolor, pastels and drawings.

The Impressionists would reside initially in Montmartre which even once they began to spread out over Paris and beyond continued to be with its cheap and bohemian living the first fertile grounds for many of the early wave of modern artists who created the cannon of great works and movements.

Henri de Toulouse-Lautrec (1864-1901) is emblematic of the bohemian Montmartrian artist in both his lifestyle and work. Although he could technically be called "Post-Impressionist" the main proponents of that loose knit group were for the most part still alive, having each individually perfected their artistic philosophy and way of working so that new movements began to spring up.

Lautrec was born in Albi (Midi-Pyreness Region of Southern France) into an aristocratic family with his father being a Comte and being descended from counts of the Toulouse and Lautrec regions of Southern France. Health problems, which it is speculated derived from his parents having been first cousins frequently kept him bedridden as a child. He would keep himself amused by drawing while stuck in bed. He received informal lessons from friend of the family René Princeteau (1844–1914) who specialized in painting sporting and society portraits. As a teen, he broke both femur bones and a hip in minor accidents. None of the injuries healed correctly and although his torso was of a normal proportion his legs development was dwarfishly stunted; making walking difficult, painful and his adult height a little under five feet.

In 1882 Lautrec moved to Paris from Albi. He studied in the ateliers of Léon Bonnat (1833–1922) and Fernand Cormon (1845–1924). Cormon would also teach Vincent van Gough (1853–1890). Shades of the impressionists, Lautrec would paint en plein air. He did not use professional models but favorite denizens of his neighborhood, usually prostitutes. Lautrec liked to use thinned out paints to keep his loose brushstrokes visible as this leant further emotion and energy to his works.

The everyday physical pain and his self-consciousness about his appearance made Lautrec a heavy drinker. The normal respectable avenues of society seemed closed off to him for all time. The good to come of him feeling so outcast was that he comfortably was able to live among the marginalized of Parisian society: the artists, streetwalkers and bohemians who would make up the larger part of the subject matter for his works. Lautrec was influenced by the impressionists in their unorthodoxy of color palettes, he transmuted the aspect of using everyday people from the naturalist/realist school, mixing it with his fascination for Japanese woodblock cuts which were also an influence for Van Gough and the composer Claude Debussy (1862-1918) to make them more stylized.

Lautrec is best known for his printmaking, especially his posters. Daumier late into his life did commercial graphic work as a means to earn a living keep the other aspect of what he did purely painterly, revolutionary in its execution and to the general public largely inaccessible. There was a populist aspect to Lautrec's work, this description not mean in a pejorative way. With his printmaking, they were often in service of advertising the newly modern nightclub life then springing up in Montmartre. Even the upper crust knew of the entertainers often referenced in his posters and often could be seen making annual sorties into the hills of Montmartre for a night of revelry.

His images for the well-known cabaret performers of the day brought him recognition and a steady stream of commissions. The first one he did for the then new Moulin Rouge (1889) was for the performer known as "La Goulue" whose real name was Louise Weber (1866-1929). She was considered the queen of Montmartre and made fashionable the can-can dance. Lautrec was innovative in his technique and choice of colors for his print work. With all his graphic work he smoothly mixed innovation with accessibility. For this poster (1891) *La Goulue* he used four separate stones and inks in black, yellow, red and blue. Additional colors were created by the layering these colors. He often also employed a technique called "crachis" (splatter) which creates mists of color similar to air brushing. This effect was achieved by shaking a brush over a sieve or running a knife along the edge of the brush to cause paint to spray. A lot of his poster work too used unorthodox compositional layouts sometimes derived from Japanese woodblock art, in how he positioned the main focal point figures. For his print of *Divan Japonais* which depicted cabaret star Yvette Gilbert who was known as "Dieuse" ("Speaker", for her style of singing) the head of the focal point is cut off yet the trademark gloves and long body let the viewer know of her identity. In the foreground was another singer Jane Avrin, (then) easily identified because of her penchant for large hats. Lautrec, like Daumier would sometimes use caricature to get to the very essence of his subjects in his graphic work.

Lautrec would participate in independent salons shows. He seems to never have felt the need for railing against any established system, be it painterly or in regard to gallery/shows. He did not have an overall cohesive artistic mission that he felt compelled to articulate and push forward into the public's consciousness. Instead he followed his own north star drawing from what came before him, new influences and his own talent perfectly capturing the zeitgeist in an artistic voice which managed to be instantly recognizable. Ill health amplified by hard living would drastically shorten his life, he was only a professional artist for little over a decade but in that time he managed to create a body of work encompassing over 1000 paintings, 275 watercolors, 5000 drawings and the over 350 prints for which he is best known.

Henri Matisse (1869-1954) said "Drawing is the intellectual basis for painting." I agree with this but it took me awhile to come to this truth. I had in a short amount of time reached the atelier of printing studio Idem Paris. The Idem Paris printing studio is one of the things which are emblematic to me of both Paris and this philosophy. They are rich in an artistic tradition without being trapped by it nor feeling the urge for any kind of artistic oedipal elimination of what came before them. Somewhat a dichotomy of words can be used when describing what still occurs in this studio, a tradition of innovation, new techniques are created but as often is the case, even with the seemingly radical young lions whose work stands the test of time, built upon or using what came before them as a jumping off point.

Idem Paris was originally known as the Mourlot Company whose affiliation with printing is important not just to Paris' printing history but that of the medium in general. Jules, the patriarch of the Mourlot family, had nine sons. In the early part of the 1900's his first shop was on the Rue Saint-Maur doing commercial work and some minor artistic prints. Even his youngest sons operated the machines learning from an early age all aspects of the art of printing. In 1914, they bought a recently closed print shop which had been run by Imprimerie Bataille on 18 Rue de Chabrol. The studio did commercial work but also the cabaret posters which had become art unto themselves thanks to the popularity of Lautrec.

Jules two eldest sons were conscripted into the war but the press remained open. Two years after his sons return Jules passed away (1921) but the sons decided to keep up the family business which was renamed

Mourlot Frères. The eldest son George handled the business aspects with the second oldest Fernand the talent and public interactions. Their younger brother Maurice painted nature scenes and still life's and would later join the company. There was a desire to elevate posters for art shows and expositions in the same manner that those of the cabarets had. In 1923 a first foray is made in an original poster for a show of modernist painter Pierre Girieud and a modernist exhibition in Copenhagen.

The book *Les Hommes Abadonnes* by humanist author Georges Duhamel (1884-1966) and featuring plates by Maurice de Vlaminck (1876-1958) was published. This book was important in that it showed a technical prowess on the part of the printers in reproducing the work of the artist. The collection of short stories also introduced a popular character of Duhamel's named Salavin. It was the start of Mourlot's receiving increased notice. Vlaminck and Maurice Utrillo (1883-1955) were given an open invitation into the printers' studio to experiment with lithography, starting the growing trend of it not merely being painting's poor relation. Before this, the normal trend was for an image done by an artist to be redone on plates or stone by a craftsman and not the artist themselves. This would make the reproduced image always pale in comparison as often the craftsmen were closer to a typesetter than an artist in temperament. The Mourlot studio also began to delve into experimenting with different types of ink and colors as to allow the prints to keep pace with painterly possibilities.

Emboldened with the growing possibilities of the medium the Mourlots accepted a commission to print lithograph posters for Muse National's hundred-year celebration of Romanticism and Delacroix (1930). They came up with the innovation that the lithographic posters should themselves be pure works of art.

In 1937 Matisse met Fernand when the studio was given the commission of supplying two posters for the Maîtres de l'Art Independent exhibition in the Petit Palais. One image was from a painting by Pierre Bonard (1867-1947) the other by him. The printed images were technically so close to those on the canvas it furthered the attention and respect of the medium. Matisse would become further intrigued by the medium. The publisher Teriade would use the printers to supply covers and visual works for several issues of their journals, many of them being by Matisse. There was never any real battle for the printers to try to break any then in place system. Like Lautrec before them, they managed to fuse a certain amount of populist element with art done as they wanted it. Mourlot would become the largest printer of art exhibition posters with museums from all over Europe engaging their services.

By the late thirties early forties, a lithographic/printing renaissance was well under way. Mourlot was printing exhibition and museum catalogs as well as posters. More artists began to come in and work in the medium. The cream of the crop out of Montparnasse, as the studio turned out not just impressive prints but also artist books too. (Alexander Calder 1898-1976, Raoul Duffy 1877-1953, Fernand Léger 1881-1955, Jean Dubuffet 1901-1985)

In October of 1945 Matisse introduced both Pablo Picasso (1881-1973) and Georges Braque (1882-1963) to the printing studio. For four months Picasso was so enamored of this new medium he would work every day from 8 AM until 8 PM. He would have a three decades long association with the Mourlots and continue graphic work for the rest of his life. Picasso was so invigorated by the possibilities of the medium that he was the most personable he had ever been to the other workers, who were not artists, in the shop shaking each one's hand good morning. Everybody was very fond of him showing complete discretion despite his already established celebrity; even as he introduced his, then *secret*, mistress Marie Therese as he slowly moved her into his number one spot.

The studio managed to underscore what was special about themselves and the medium by the diversity of artists who worked there, the collaborations fostered between artists and authors and the total sense of freedom. There was never a sense of limitation in the technical sense as printing rules were frequently broken to be replaced by innovation. The most skilled craftsman in the shop, Monsieur Tutin would print up Picasso's work. There was such an unorthodoxy in what Picasso wanted to do even as he ignored the established rules. Every piece to be printed was accompanied by seduction on Picasso's part. As much as Picasso teased him, every piece turned out as he envisioned them spurring him onto great experimentation and confirming his faith in Monsieur's skill.

By the mid-forties, the studio was not only recognized as the first to make the medium a serious artistic one but also the best. The Communist Peace Conference was being held in Paris in 1949. Picasso was asked to supply an image for the poster. His friend, the poet Louis Aragon a figure of growing power in the communist party was asked to facilitate. Picasso was used to honors and attentions and even as he continued working in the studio had nothing specific ready. Aside from typical absorption in his work his enthusiasm was most likely tempered by the fact that writers who had been in his circle but dropped or he had cooled on such as Aragon and (poet) Paul Eluard (1895-1952) had become war heroes and politically active in the party not needing nor trying to curry favor with the master. Picasso also was never as politically astute as he would like people to believe but knew to pass on the honor could make it so that it was offered to an artistic rival.

After being politely put off after many inquiries about an image Aragon flipped through a large portfolio at the studio. He found a print of a white pigeon, the type typical of the south with a frilly neck and long feathers covering the feet which could easily be confused for a dove. The real bird had been given to Picasso by Matisse who had always been fond of birds. Initially upon receiving the gift Picasso wondered if Matisse were mocking him but decided to accept the gift anyways as he felt it may allow him to absorb a spark from Matisse. The image is now a very familiar one done with fluidic but minimal amount of lines.

From artists who had to flee Paris during the war to post war collectors and visitors to Paris the legitimacy of prints as a complex medium unto itself became clearer. Print makers with no commercial concerns but only artistic goals have sprung up worldwide. What is interesting is there are no hard and fast "schools" stylistically. One could do a cubist painting now but that specific genres day has come and gone and at best a cubist executed canvas now has the unspoken subtext of being done "in the style of". Whereas printmaking still has technical innovations for materials and technique but is not trapped nor defined by them. Inherently there is more freedom to be had still.

I feel in full communion with my adopted city right now not worrying about the legacy or fate of my own work. The Mourlot Company moved in 1976 to the building I now stand before, 49 Rue du Montparnasse. Originally Emile Dufrenoy built the place to house his printing and lithographic presses. I step through the doors into a mall inner courtyard.

From the 1930's until the mid-70's The Michard Printing Company who specialized in printing geographical maps occupied the current space. In 1976 Mourlot Printing Studio took over the space. There are two floors, about 15,000 square feet. The atelier is filled up but does not feel cluttered. There is not the feeling of an oppressive shrinking space which a tinkerer's warren slowly morphs into. A necropsied museum as one unused thing covers another forgotten one. There is dust in the corners but it is not the detritus of disuse but merely the equivalent of architectural sweat from a place still very much in use.

The ground floor has Voirin and Marinoni flatbed machines which are from the 19th century, powered by gas and steam boilers and operated with a pulley system. I touch each in turn for luck the way one would nod to a mountain or the ocean. These beasts look not so much still as merely sleeping. In 1997 Fernand's son Jacque retired and the name of the company was changed to the now familiar one of Idem Paris. The second floor has smaller presses to make test pressings and after chatting briefly with some artists making prints I let myself out as to not be a nuisance.

I head home. The second floor also has a series of small studios, I tell myself it is a new ambition to work there but even if I never have the chance it is all right we are all connected.

I put some Bud Powell on and knock out some more pieces. I do a few of Dina, based off of sketches and memory, in gray and blue wash. If I have more than the commission calls for, will that temper my achievement or seem an even better thing to Michael? No matter how good one was at something there was suspicion if it appeared too easy to an onlooker regardless of the countless hours put in to achieve that ease.

I would give myself two weeks, do as may pieces as I wanted and then cherry pick the best from the batch with but two extra per series. I continued on using Dina as a model. We reverted to using my studio but one sunny morning to break things up we used my apartment, this time with her on the overstuffed chair which the previous tenant had left because of its weight. Sitting sideways, one padded arm supported her back the other held her legs up from behind her knees. I was seeing her but as I would anyone when in the midst of working. For her part, the sun even with the uncomfortable position had lulled her into a stupor. Almost finished with the main lines of her body she began to come back into focus as a person. Her belly had a crease in it and every curved surface from there to breasts to cheeks to eyelids had a pinkish blush to them. She came out of it at almost the same time as me, catching my gaze peripherally she laughed and said;

"Intimate huh?"

HOUSE OF POETS: RUSSIAN CLASSICAL MUSIC

It had been another hot day. I showered and this gave the illusion of the air having cooled down but this temporary comfort also disguised the inadequate job that I had done of drying off.

I did not discover this until after getting under the sheets. They clung to the back of my legs and my shoulders. It made me dream that I was on a ship with a woman whom I did not care about. The both of us having stubbornly remained together despite all the years of having made each other miserable.

I woke up. It was hours until dawn. The water had long ago dried up only to be replaced now by the dampness of perspiration. A light floral note, violets, mixed with the bleach like note of the detergent which the concierge had supplied and that tomorrow I must replace with one possessing a less institutional bouquet.

If I lay not on my back but rather on my side, then the detergent's bleach note dominated. As sleep once again retook me, I wondered if it would have been worse had I dreamed of the hospital instead.

My day started out well enough. I had done some good work early in the morning but knew that I had to tackle some of the business side of things after lunch. It is not having a strong desire to please causing me, when I say that I will do something whether it is mailing out slides of my latest pieces or really, anything else, to be Johnny on the spot.

The life of an artist is nothing like its portrayal in the media, in regard to day to day existence. As wrong as the movies and television get that, the business side, although rarely shown, is portrayed with even more inaccuracies. An important aspect of being a full time working artist involves a non-creative collaboration which must take place with gallerists, collectors.

Regardless of how organized, ambitious or talented one is, there exists the ankle weight of others having to do their part too. Even though they too do not get paid until all aspects of a show is done, "partners" often do their part in a sort of inattentive and overly casual tempo. They must be chased down and borderline harassed to sign things, confirm things, ship things out.

Of course, it is a matter of what one wants as far as a career goes. I have known many good painters who are stuck at one level but as they no longer need do anything save their art to eat, are perfectly happy.

It is not quite a myth: the archetype of the artist who only creates and has coterie of clipboard carrying assistants taking care of every other detail of their life but that is rarefied upper strata of artists and chances are that at least some of them spent their early years staying on top of all the aggravating business matters.

The rest of my day is spent doling out reminders to people of what they need to be doing, now late.

When I had first started, I would aspire for any exposure of my work. Having achieved an audience and pedigree, there must now be a matching appropriate level to where my work will appear. The currency I assign my own work will dictate how it is perceived. Naively, I used to think that it was all about talent. The politics of it did not matter as far as sales or placement went. Very quickly those who stay in the game realize this is not how it is played though.

Even with all I have under my belt, nothing is ever guaranteed. New galleries, collectors and journalists often like to see me jump through hoops upon initial contact, it is part of the game. Impulse control now more reigned in, my patience and forced humility in these things garner me better results; although occasionally I do miss a good anger jag publicly vented.

For the rest of the day I vacillate between angst and joy. It is not a matter of always looking on the bright side, which seems to me somewhat of an idiot mantra, so much as keeping things in perspective. Even with all the terrible business side of it. I am doing good work, free to explore and follow my own North star.

I go to bed, a mix of sweet and sour on my tongue.

I look out the window as I sip my coffee. The unfastened belt of my bathrobe hangs down on either side of me, the cut strings of a puppet. Cream up in the sky, slowly drifting towards the mountains. They might get the rain but not here at their feet. This is all right as otherwise it would have been too easy to spend the day in bed with Turgenev.

Sitting at my table, the pencil birthing worlds, I stop but only to put some music on. I want to choose something that is not what I usually reach for as to really hear it and not merely have it be on in the background serving as a mere part of my ritual.

Marina had told me that I had a Russian soul; that in a past life it had been very hard and my reward was to have now found myself rebirthed in the city of trees, with its public parks and the little artificial ponds in which happily splash the turtles.

My records are organized by genre for jazz and by nation for classical. I knew another collector who went a step further creating subcategories by generation, both of us laughing as I said;

"That is crazy."

My mind flashes to the calls I must make but can put off at least until the end of the week. All my Russian heroes in literature and music, they had it far worse than I. To delve into their lives, their vowel rich names become a litany of perseverance. I pull several down off the shelf. As if planning a feast, I arrange the small pile in *proper order* as their work came into the world.

Unlike almost any other nation, Russia's classical music does not have a formalized tradition with various eras (baroque, classical, romantic et al) that goes back hundreds of years in the same way as other countries do.

It would continue to grow but in its nascent stage, the initial history and establishment happened over a mere seventy years or so. To someone who is more than a casual listener but not a full on academic, when thinking of maverick composers, often the second Viennese School comes to mind (Schoenberg 1874-1951, Webern 1874-1945, Berg 1885-1935).

As radical as the oeuvres of these composers may seem, all had formalized musical education which gave them foundations to build off and to reject as they innovated new techniques.

The early wave of Russian composers were all to varying degree autodidactic. This was largely more freeing than limiting. A degree from any good university or conservatory is impressive, however the advantage often to be found with autodidacts is that they are pursuing their knowledge on their own accord and so remain unwaveringly engaged. This continues to be true even today.

There had been symphonic/chamber and opera music in Russia before the advent of the first great Russian composers but it was largely foreign music from Italy and France. There was a small body of comic opera based off Russian librettos, although not always by Russians.

Mikhail Glinka (1804-1857) was the progenitor of the idea for a Russian Nationalist school (aesthetic). During this time, to be nationalist was more in line with a type of programmatic aesthetic, the term not having sinister connotations until the 20th century.

Glinka came from a well-off family. At the age of ten while listening to an uncle's private orchestra he became interested in music. The first lessons he received was from his governess. After this, there were general studies at the chief pedagogic institute in St. Petersburg (1818-22). He also took piano lessons from the Irish composer/pianist John Field (1782-1837) who was part of the city's artistic society.

Religious music and folk songs aside, it was only the upper classes who had exposure to music on a regular basis. The great houses would import/sponsor virtuosos from other countries and create their own private orchestras. There was, even among some of the royalty a legitimate enthusiasm for music. Empress Anna Ivanovna had imported an Italian opera troupe to entertain her court. Enthusiasm for sponsorship of a virtuoso or creating any kind of philharmonic Orchestra aside, they were still looked at as merely another thing to show off to one's peers.

Unlike, as example, Germany though there were no major systems in place for composers to work up the ranks and achieve titled positions. This is one of the reasons why the first wave of Russian composers all had other careers not affiliated with their artistic lives. Glinka had an advantage of coming from a titled family which further took pressure off thoughts of rebelling or having to concentrate mainly on earning a living.

Glinka absorbed more of the flavor of his beloved country while doing a tour which despite its louche fashion, made an impression upon him. He ended it at some of his family's estates where he further delved into self-study of music.

He ended his exile and found himself working for four years at the ministry of education. Even though he was not interested in an official career, the artistic, city life greatly appealed to him. While living a cosmopolitan life, he interacted with some of the cream of artistic society including authors Leo Tolstoy (1828-1910) and Alexander Pushkin (1799-1837). This intellectual stimulation would serve to help form him as an artist.

His musical studies also continued, taken in haphazard manner. The initial compositions to emerge from his pen were small pieces, chamber and songs. They showed a strong influence of what he admired from the French and German composers.

Feeling worn out, Glinka left his ministry job and decided to go to Italy. During the three years he spent in Italy he struck up acquaintances with and became passionate about the music of Vincenzo Bellini (1801-35) and Gaetano Donizetti (1797-1848). So deeply did Glinka delve into their works, that they overly flavored his own work. As he lived through his self-imposed exile, a feeling of being homesick began to emerge.

As he contemplated home he continued to absorb Italian music. Being in the country in which the two composers lived and wrote, Glinka noticed how their work seemed to radiate the spirit of their country. We carry our homes within us, in the food that we cook and the songs that we sing. This became apparent during his exile. Glinka's nostalgia for home and the example set by his Italian peers served to articulate within his mind the idea of creating a markedly Russian music. Nationalistic, in subject and style.

Even once Glinka established his artistic métier, he would still allow some Italian and French influences into his work. His programmatic conceptions would have more far reaching effect than his compositional devices.

In 1833, he studied under Siegfried Dehn (1799-1858). Dehn was a great theorist, teacher and librarian. He brought back attention to both J.S Bach (1685-1750) who had fallen well out of vogue and Orlando di Lasso (1532-1594) who had been wholly forgotten. This was Glinka's first serious study. Before this all his lessons and learning had been very haphazard. A year into his studies, the death of his father forced his return to Russia.

Back in Russia he got married but never mentioned to his new wife his non-desire to change. They brought out the worst in each other with his wife becoming bitter and nagging in response to his behavior. He composed *A Life for the Tsar* over the course of two years which put their widening rift on the backburner. This premiered in 1836 with the Imperial family in attendance. This opera brought him the first flush of fame. Stylistically he still showed signs of other nation's influences but mixed in were innovations which allowed for greater unity of drama and music. Subject wise, it was the start of nationalistic theme which would be picked up by the next wave of composers. The patriotic theme of the work ensured that the audience would be engaged while also insulating it against any kind of imperial disapproval for its progressive sonics.

Spurred on not only by his work's popularity but also further cohesion of his ideas, Glinka also wrote some of his best songs during this period.

His second opera took a long time to complete, hampered by a lack of strong work ethos and trouble with the libretto. Compounding the difficulties were troubles with his health and marriage.

Ruslan and Lyudmila was based off a poem by Pushkin, whose death prevented him from writing the libretto. Sonically, this was a more adventurous work. Rather than incorporating in elements from western classical tradition, Glinka drew from some eastern colorations.

It premiered in 1842 with the cream of society in attendance, including the Tsar's family. The experimental nature of the music did not appeal to the crowd. Plot wise, while not political opera, some parts could be interpreted as overtly commenting upon the Tsar's divine right to rule. The royal family left the event noticeably early.

This second opera proved to be a public and critical failure. The disappointment with it was not total. Within this opera could be found the template which the next wave of composers would build off of.

Glinka's marriage broke up, with his wife remarrying without first seeking a divorce. It added to the bitterness he felt from the failure of his opera. The mounting disappointment served as the motivation for him to leave Russia in 1844.

Just as they had musically, Italy and France would have importance in his self-imposed exile. In Paris, he became close to quintessential romantic era composer, Hector Berlioz (1803-69). Glinka would try to promote his friend's work back home. It was under Berlioz that in 1845 Glinka's work premiered, the first wholly Russian music to be performed in the west.

For the rest of his life, Glinka would work sporadically. He spent some time in Spain (1845-7) studying Spanish music and composing some pieces which incorporated or were inspired by local flavor ("Two Spanish Overtures", "Aragonese Jota", "Summer Night in Madrid").

Travel seemed necessary for his creative process. There was the pursuit of an unknown thing, which once caught or harnessed could change everything for him. This chase was more on subconscious level, never receiving his full attention but existing more as an ambient prodding into action.

Being away from home allowed him to crystalize its essence in his head, the picture coming into sharper focus in direct proportion to his homesickness. Yet, home also meant intrigues and conflict along with other distractions which effected his work.

Frequently, Glinka would find himself back in Paris, whose cultural appeals never waned for him. His years abroad were halted once again by forces outside of his control, this time the Crimean War.

Returning to Russia Glinka wrote his memoirs, *Zapiski*. This memoir was first published in St. Petersburg in 1887 surprised society with both his wit and accurate picture he painted of himself, defects and all.

Glinka decided to return to Germany and his studies with Dehn. Upon arriving, he became seriously ill, passing away shortly after.

A perpetuated shorthand in describing him, which persists to this day, is that of a "dilettante of genius". This over simplifies the matter. The trajectory of his career and even his reputation in the West was hampered by several factors.

There was his lax work ethos which also dictated the size of his oeuvre. Even within the tradition of great Western Composers, those with smaller bodies of work tend to fall by the wayside with the passage of time.

Both his production and appreciation were affected by the fact that he was creating something brand new with no steadfast steps for him to take regarding what to write, when. The importance of creating a nationalist (musical) aesthetic would live on past him but he did not work at evolving and growing it in a singular fashion. As much as the initial conception was his alone, his works do not all speak of it

In 1848 Glinka wrote *Kamarinskaya*. Tchaikovsky would say;

"This was the acorn from which the oak of later Russian symphonic music grew."

This piece was as important as the idea of (musical) nationalism for providing a type of template. It is based off two well-known folk melody/songs, a bridal song and a dance piece. Structurally, it does not have the same tension-release as was found in Western Classical music. There would often within the works of Glinka's direct artistic descendants be folkloric elements, whether an appropriation of musical structures or myths/fables. Glinka's piece showed the way to a musical nationalism not just in a work's program but also by incorporating a region's folk forms.

The next wave of Russian composers would take aspects of what Glinka had done as a starting point to build off. His second opera had fantasy/folkloric elements within the plot which would be a major feature of compositions from the next group of composers. The other important element which Glinka utilized in his second opera was the technique of playing classical elements off eastern ("oriental") devices (rhythms and scales) as opposed to traditional European ones. This exoticism would be greatly identified with Russian classical music that was about to emerge.

Glinka was still alive at the advent of the next wave of Russian composers. They were directly inspired by his example, building off it. Their chief progenitor, Mily Balakirev (1837-1910) would have some interactions with him.

Russian society, pre-revolution would have one eye progressively towards the future while the other remained steeped in the repetition of tradition. Which aspects were in the foreground depend upon who was on the throne. This dichotomy would allow for more possibilities in the arts without the outright censure which would often occur later.

Balakirev came from a working-class family in Nizhny Novgorod. With a nod towards more bourgeoisie social aspirations, his mother began teaching him piano at the age of four. He took to it and maintained an interest so that at the age of ten she took him to Moscow for an intensive series of ten lessons with Alexander Dubuque. Dubuque himself was a student of ex-pat pianist/composer John Field who would teach some of Balakirev's future musical collaborators.

Returning home, he continued his studies until the death of his mother. After that he boarded at school (Alexandrovsky Institute). His burgeoning musical talent caught the attention of Count Alexander Ulybyshev, a local leading light of the town's musical life.

Ulybyshev had written books on Mozart and Beethoven and possessed a large and diverse musical library. He had already been affiliated with the pianist Karl Eisrach to whom he was a patron. Eisrach also took notice of Balakirev's talent

The two took it upon themselves to further his musical education. It was arranged for Balakirev to give musical performances and he was introduced to the works of Chopin and Glinka. Like a lot of upper class houses, Ulybyshev had his own private orchestra. Balakirev was often allowed to conduct the rehearsals for them. When he was only fourteen he led a performance of Mozart's *Requiem.*

A year later he led rehearsals for both Beethoven's first and eighth symphonies. He also began writing his own compositions which included "A Grande Fantasy on Russian Folksongs for Piano and Orchestra".

Later, when Balakirev gathered around him other likeminded composers to formally create a group, he would initially be the only professional composer. Back in 1853 he started attending the University of Kazan as a mathematics student.

While immersed in his studies he participated in the local music scene as a pianist. He also kept involved with music by earning some extra money teaching piano.

During holiday breaks, he would go back to his patron's estate where his own writing further progressed. Once his studies were completed his patron took him to Saint Petersburg in 1855.

It was here that he got to meet Glinka. From their initial meeting, Glinka transmitted a passion for the nascent idea of a purely Russian music.

Despite some minor criticism of the works he was shown, Glinka nurtured the idea of his taking up the life of a professional composer. To underscore his confidence Glinka gave him two melodies which he had written in Spain before once again departing for the west. Balakirev used them both creating "Spanish Serenade for Strings" and "Overture on a Spanish March".

A year into his life in Saint Petersburg, Balakirev made his musical debut playing his own work. He also played the piano part of Beethoven's "Emperor Concerto" for the Tsar. Even with his growing notice and the publication of twelve songs, he was barely staying financially afloat. A mixed blessing was the lifeline of giving piano lessons and playing balls, which kept him exhausted but also from starving.

In one rough year Balakirev lost both his patron and Glinka. He had already been enthused about the concept of a Russian aesthetic. With Glinka now gone, he felt that it was his responsibility to take up the mantle of facilitator as to make it a reality.

Initially, Balakirev formed a group to further his mission made up of theorists and critics. It was realized that there was a need for more than just himself composing.

The critic Vladimir Stasov (1824-1906) was a holdover from the first group which had formed. The group of composers which gathered around Balakirev gave a concert of original music for Slav envoys. In writing a positive review he gave the group its moniker The Mighty Handful.

Over the course of the group's span it would also be referred to as "The Five" and "The New Russian School". Stasov helped articulate their mission and initially could almost be considered the behind the scenes sixth member. One of their tenets was a rejection of formal learning. Balakirev was virulently anti-formalized learning. As Russia during this time had no conservatory system, this would not be too hard a rule for members of the group to obey. In their unorthodoxy and temperaments, plus the rejection of institutionalized learning, "The New Russian School" seems almost contrary a title. "The Mighty Handful" is probably the most apt.

All the Mighty Handful were to varying degrees, autodidactic. Some of their compositional uniqueness and the distinctive individuality can be attributed to this.

It is easy, down the corridor of time to try to asses each composer via posthumous reputation, technical weaknesses, and stylistic innovation. This is to miss the point. There was no member more important or greater than another, all were links in a rapidly forged chain.

Balakirev could be overly pedantic in how he viewed the manner in which the group should compose. At first it seemed an ideal guidance to help with direction. Eventually though, it would be felt as an unneeded repression. For this burgeoning group, ultimately their commonality was not in style but in goal.

There is often an unintentional tradition with artists and theorists in any medium and era who form a group to create something brand new. They are united first by the desire to do something as yet unheard of. Then a further bond is created via the commonality of seeking, if not acceptance then understanding and exposure of their works to society at large. Personalities and the pressures of where to go once the initial goal is accomplished becomes a source of tension which, even when personal friendships remain, become terminal for a group as a whole.

After first inspiring each other, helping to forge something new, the members all started to think past their initial mission statement. Former allies would find themselves critical enemies in the way that only former friends can ever be.

Balakirev's association with critics and theorists was of great help in honing his artistic mission's structure. Ideas without anyone to carry them out risk disappearing. Balakirev needed composers to join him in creating works along the line of his nationalistic idea.

Cesar Cui (1835-1918) was the first composer to join the collective. Cui's music would be the least Russian out of all the members of the group. Glinka had been inspired by Paris and to an even larger extent so would Cesar.

He may have inherently been receptive to a French influence as his father had been a French officer under Napoleon during the emperor's campaign of 1812. Having first been a prisoner, he elected to stay in Russia after the war.

Cui's mother was Lithuanian (then part of Russian Empire) and he spent his early life there. While very young he had composition lessons and started writing music with Chopin being a big stylistic influence.

In 1851, he went to St. Petersburg to attend the school of

engineering. Four years later he began studying at the academy of military engineering. His talent was such that by 1857 he was giving lectures which led to a full professor position in fortifications in 1878. By the end of his military career he would retire with the rank of lieutenant general (1906).

All during his military teaching career which also included onsite inspections, Cui kept up his musical writing. In the span of his musical career he wrote fifteen operas. Like other members of The Mighty Handful, Pushkin was a source touchstone. He also utilized the writings of Victor Hugo (1802-1885), Alexander Dumas (1802-1870), Guy de Maupassant (1850-1893) and Prosper Merimee (1802-70).

Whereas the other members of the group drew ideas from the land and folkloric elements, Franz Liszt (1811-1886) was an important figure from which he drew. His work was the least nationalistic of the group and could be seen to be closer to the French symbolist stylistically.

Cui also wrote many articles and music/performance reviews. In the early years of his writing, he had to keep them anonymous because of his military career. His non-de plume was three asterisks but everyone in St. Petersburg knew it was him. Between 1864 to 1918 he wrote some 800 articles often for the St. Petersburg news. He also wrote books on military fortifications which quickly became standards.

His biting critiques caused blowback when his own works were performed. Even with his criticisms alienating some, he was awarded membership in several prestigious musical societies outside of Russia. The Académie Française made him a correspondent and awarded him the cross of the Legion d' Honneur. The Belgium academy of Literature and art made him a member in 1896.

By 1900 he would retire from doing regular music criticism but continued to write about music. In his long view of history, he would dismiss everything which came before Beethoven, including Mozart. His rapier pen had cost him some support over the years but never everything. Occasionally his pen would be turned onto fellow members of his group which would be cutting but without the same rancor. Even when divisively criticizing allies, he also did gestures of support.

Cui gave up his chair on the selection committee for the Marinsky Theater in 1893 along with fellow Handful member Rimsky-Korsakov over the rejection of their compatriot Mussorgsky's work *Khovanshchina*. He would also honor past allegiances after the group broke up by completing Mussorgsky's opera *The Fair at Sorochyntsi.*

In the West, more of his music is now available than ever before. Yet he is still known mostly for a handful of smaller pieces, especially "Orientale" (op 50 no 9) for piano and violin. Stylistically, his music does not give the air of having sprung richly up from Russian soil.

Cui did not possess the sui generis of Mussorgsky or the tonal complexity of Rimsky-Korsakov but he was an important promoter of Russian music to the West.

Cui was less concerned with the Russian programmatic part of their creed than that of anti-formalism aspect. During the time that the group was a cohesive whole, and afterwards an important factor for him was that of the autodidactic.

Among all five though, his may have been the least Russian but would also be the closest to the next wave which started with Pytor Ilyich Tchaikovsky (1840-1893) whose career began around the same time that Russia began a formalized conservatory system close to the German manner.

This would become a sort of Russian romanticism which would slowly morph into a combination of The Mighty Handful's idea of Russian music but as perceived by the West's ideas of its people and lands. An induced artificiality of melancholy melodies, onion domed churches, murderous royalty and enchantments.

Alexander Borodin (1883-87) occupies the middle of The Mighty Handful. To the causal listener he is not as obscure as Cui and Balakirev. Borodin has several works known to concert goers, the lesser amount keeping his reputation from being on par with the other two members whose works are now ostensibly part of the classical cannon, Rimsky-Korsakov and Mussorgsky.

Borodin did not present specific technical innovations to be built off of. Instead he furthered the cause of creating a new nationalistic genre.

He was born the illegitimate son of Prince Luke Ghedeanishvili, descendant of Caucasian Royalty. His mother was middle class wife of a physician. As was the custom, the baby was registered under the name of the prince's head serf; "Borodin".

Borodin's father died when he was only seven, his mother took over raising him. She was cultured and sensitive, at times overly so. He was a frail child and she was convinced that he had TB. In fear of for his health he had four years of not attending school, receiving instead a series of tutors.

The house in which he grew up was one of almost exclusively women. Occasionally, he referred to himself as a girl. Even as a child Borodin showed himself to be not only highly intelligent but possessing an impressive retentive memory. He also had an aptitude for language, science and music.

The first musical memories were hearing music drift into his window of a military band playing in their barracks. He struck up an acquaintance with some of the musicians and took flute lessons. With proficiency quickly achieved as a musician he wrote his first piece of music, a polka, at the age of nine. It was inspired by a love affair with a mature woman.

Music continued to hold his interest and he became friends with the child prodigy Misha Shchiglev. Using piano, they explored classical music while furthering their knowledge by also attending concerts.

The two friends taught themselves how to play stringed instruments as to allow them to join chamber ensembles. For them both, there was an addictive quality to their musical participation. In any type of weather, they would walk the seven miles to perform.

Borodin's immersion into music began to include more composition. During this time of early adolescence, he wrote a concerto for flute and piano and a string trio based on a theme from Giacomo Meyerbeer's (1791-1864) *Robert le Diable*.

Even with all of his musical activity, he kept up with scientific education. Chemistry was his primary interest but in his era there was a prerequisite of a medical foundation too.

To be able to move forward into his chosen field at the age of seventeen he enrolled in the Academy of Medicine and Surgery, specializing in botany and chemistry.

His school career was filled with honor after honor. With his reputation for brilliance he was appointed assistant professor of pathology and therapeutics in 1856, two years after this he earned his medical degree.

Borodin's mentor, professor Zinin decided upon his direction in research rather than a medical practice. Zinin sent him to Heidelberg, Germany to further his studies in 1859. It was while in Heidelberg that Borodin met the woman whom he would eventually marry.

Catherine Protopopova was a pianist too. She introduced Borodin to the works of Schumann and Chopin. She also helped Borodin maintain interest and involvement in the musical world while he pursued his other studies.

He would bring her back to Russia where they married. The couple moved into in an apartment at the Academy of Medicine in St. Petersburg. This would be the address that they would share for the rest of their lives.

Back in Russia while still growing accustomed to his new life, science took up more of his time. Borodin published a series on important papers and made some valuable scientific discoveries as compensation for a drop down in musical activity.

His growing renown earned him the position of lecturer at the St. Petersburg Academy of Forestry and as a professor at the Academy of Medicine.

During all this activity, although diminished in the time he could devote to it, there was still the musical side of his life too. With music, he viewed himself as an accomplished and passionate hobbyist. Borodin found satisfaction in being able to play and compose as his schedule allowed. There was never any angst in the desire to be able to free himself as to be able to pursue his muse.

Borodin found himself falling into Balakirev's orbit in 1869. Their interactions served as a catalyst for Borodin to begin emphasizing composing over merely performing.

Furthering his musical studies with Balakirev, Borodin started to compose his first symphony. Being new to the process, added to which was his other life in science, made it a slow-going ordeal.

Despite the slowness of execution, Borodin found the task personally rewarding. The association with Balakirev brought him into contact with the rest of The Mighty Handful. Their artistic mission and its accompanying aesthetic appealed to him. Borodin was absorbed into the group which became The Mighty Handful. Sharing in their Nationalistic mission gave his work a concrete purpose behind it, making conceptualization easier.

The first symphony was completed in 1867. It fit in with the group's nascent mission. For the premier in 1869, Balakirev conducted. The audience reaction and interest went towards furthering the groups' cause.

The positive experience had Borodin planning for his next symphony. His other life and the speed in which he worked made it so that it took nine years to complete. In the interim he wrote easier to finish songs.

He also wrote the score for a comic opera *The Bogatyrs*. This work was still within the tenets of the group, Bogatyrs figuring into Russian epics.

The opera was staged uncredited (1867) but was disregarded after a very short run. It would be forgotten until 1936. It would then be brought back in Moscow only to be quickly banned for what was perceived as criticism of Russian social mores.

Even with the increased formal importance of music for him, Borodin did not abandon science. While working slowly on the second symphony he founded medical courses for women. Borodin also created a free laboratory for poor science students.

The laboratories at the academy needed to become more up to date. As to ensure that this was done in the best possible manner, he set out on an exhaustive reconnaissance of labs in Germany.

With all his activity, the second symphony was not completed until 1876. It suffered from two major problems. The actual performance was lackluster and being an autodidactic, some of the score's wind section parts were weak. Without any tricks of the trade as traditional music student would have had there was no spackle for the holes.

The disappointment was not any kind of deterrent, ill effects probably tempered by the speed in which he worked. Undeterred, he wrote some smaller pieces. "On the Steppes of Central Asia", one of his best-known pieces was completed in 1880. This piece was fully realized, utilizing theories which had long been in discussion among Borodin's group.

This piece also contains moments of an underlying exoticism which would become prominently associated with Russian classical music in the minds of Westerners.

Borodin was also working on his second-string quartet at this time which took him seven years to complete and leans more towards the romantic tradition as already existing in Western Europe.

Prince Igor could easily be said to be Borodin's most important work. Being based off historic and folkloric elements, it fit organically into the group's philosophy. There were also forward-thinking elements which in their originality belonged solely to Borodin.

The idea for the opera came about in 1869, from talks of Russian history with Stasov who still was in association with the group. It was Stasov who initially suggested Prince Igor as subject.

In conversation with Borodin, Stasov would describe landscapes, narrative episodes and the drama which could then frame it all. After massive research Borodin wrote the libretto himself. He slowly had morphed it from its initial dramatic conception into one more epic in nature.

Because it had initially started as a drama, there is a greater emotional complexity in the epic's characters. Using a figure who had moved from history into legend allowed for criticism and discussion of where Russia was intellectually and politically and where it should strive to go. It was among other things, a call to enlightenment.

He worked on this opera the rest of his life, although not non-stop. Even with his immersive enthusiasm, he never completed it. The opera would be finished by fellow group member Rimsky-Korsakov and Glazunov, premiering in St. Petersburg in 1890.

Towards the end of Borodin's life his wife was seriously ill almost perpetually. He himself got cholera in 1884. His mother in law whom he had liked died shortly after this. It led to a depression he tried to fight through by working on his opera and third symphony.

Even with his emotional and physical setbacks his home became an epicenter of socializing. Borodin would drink gallons of tea while lots of people were perpetually coming and going. There would be strangers sleeping on floors, in the bathtub. New faces engaging him in light conversation across from the dinner table.

Borodin liked the stimulation and enjoyed the unending companionship. It was also a way for him to never become a slave to the score sheets.

His wife's illness made her become a little eccentric, exasperated by their home life style. She developed bad insomnia. He tried to arrange their lives to her clock, eating wrong meals at odd hours.

Even with the unorthodoxy of his later life there was not a tragic element to it as existed with some of his peers.

The night of his death, Borodin had attended a ball at the Academy. He was dressed in full national costume. Amidst laughing, dancing and having a great time he collapsed, his friends at first thinking it a joke. An aneurism painlessly killing him during all the merriment.

With his compositions, Borodin initially showed a strong influence from German romanticism. After becoming enmeshed with the philosophy of his peers his music moved away from being made up mostly of traceable preexisting elements.

Borodin's music drew from the melodic devices of Russian church music and folkloric melodies. He combined these though with a high degree of exoticism from the East. The latter often being in a higher proportion than what sprang up from his native soil.

If Cui was the least nationalistic in some of his compositions programs, then Borodin could be said to be the least programmatic. Some of his works could be categorized as "pure music" in the vein of his friend and hero, Franz Liszt. Yet these were not anathema to the group as they still often sought to portray a feeling of Russia and Russian things, just not necessarily as specific.

His contributions would be felt, even if indirectly by the next wave of composers and in how Russian Classical music was thought of in the West with its whiffs of exotic perfumes and fairy tale like castles.

Although his reputation is not as "obscure" as his fellow Handful members: Cui and Borodin, Modest Mussorgsky's work was negatively viewed in the 19th century. He was the vodka fueled primitive whose works contained the kernel of something good which needed to be corrected as to properly come to the fore. Deeper study over the passage of time has begun to rehabilitate the many inaccuracies of initial assessments of his oeuvre.

Modest's (1839-1881) father had been a landowner, while his father's grandmother had been a serf. His own mother had artistic leanings playing piano well and giving Modest his first lessons at the age of seven.

What as an adult he would consider a lynchpin moment was when his nurse introduced him to Russian folklore. His deep interest and affection for the materials would go towards greatly contributing to his artistic aesthetic.

As he delved deeper into ethnic source materials his desire to create a national music which embodied the people and where they lived grew.

There had always been certain trajectories in other countries for artists to take: the grand tour, apprenticing and conservatory. However,

Russia did not have a conservatory system in place at this time and the children of upper middle class, especially males had other established trajectories which they were expected to take. Usually these paths led to a career in government of the military.

In 1849 Modest was taken to St. Petersburg to attend the Peter-Paul School in preparation for a military career. Even while preparing for the practical considerations of Modest's future, his father did not disapprove of his musical aptitude. He arranged lessons for his son with Anton Gerke who would later become the professor of music at the Saint Petersburg Conservatory.

By 1852 he was in the school for cadets. While there he wrote his first composition, a polka titled "Podpraporschik". Modest's father paid to publish it. During his academic career, Modest showed himself to be intelligent and intellectually curious but undisciplined. This attitude combined with alcohol would be his rhythm in later life, work, punctuated by benders.

The Preobrazhensky Guards were formed by Peter the Great (1672-1725). It was one of the oldest imperial guard regiments. By 1819 it was made up solely of young aristocrats. Modest was a lieutenant in the guards in 1856. He became friends with some fellow officers who were Italian music aficionados and future group partner Borodin.

Modest's regimental commander introduced him to the composer Alexander Dargomyzhsky. He established himself within the musical milieu attending musical evenings and through this socialization discovered the music of Glinka.

In 1859, he saw the Kremlin for the first time. Afterwards he would say;

"It represented my physical communion with Russian history."

His other artistic touchstone was meeting and starting to study with Balakirev.

There occurred a chain of events which dictated the trajectory of the rest of Modest's life. After the death of his father in 1853, he and his brother saw a serious loss of money due to the mismanagement of their patrimony. Throughout Russia serfs were freed which impacted their income further and what little was left of their money vanished.

Modest quit the army to devote himself to music. The privation and seemingly endless harangues from money lenders to whom he was in debt quickly made him start working as a civil servant in the ministry of communication (1863).

During this time of change and hardship Modest would reach his artistic maturity (1866) writing a song collection about regular people:

"Darling Savistwa", "Hopak", "The Seminarist".

A year later he would release an even larger collection of songs. Like all the rest of The Mighty Handful, Modest was an autodidactic. Part of his individuality would come from his foundationless unorthodoxy but he did also learn by doing. The song writing emboldened him to write a symphonic poem "Night on Bald Mountain".

By 1868 he was at the height of his artistic powers writing the song cycle *Detskaya* (The Nursery) and a few scenes from Gogol's *The Marriage*.

The Marriage was to be an opera whose source material was from the great Russian author but whose libretto Modest would write himself. Russian folklore would often be used for a device of the burgeoning nationalistic genre. Modest considered naturalism a complimentary accoutrement. He wanted characters to speak in a naturalistic way and mix satire with pathos. He would abandon this project before completing it but had learned enough in its initial execution to want to take up attempting an opera again.

After his mother died in 1865 he first lived with his brother then he shared a flat with fellow 'Handful member Rimsky-Korsakov. They would be roommates until 1872. Despite being moody and needy, Rimsky-Korsakov only moved out on account of getting married.

The drama by Pushkin *Boris Godunov* was Modest's next attempt at opera for which he tackled the libretto himself (1869). The first version was rejected by the advisory committee to the imperial theater for not having a prima donna role.

Over the next few years he would write major revisions. In 1872, he added new episodes and the characters of Marina and Rangoni. After further tweaking, it had its premiere in 1874 to great success.

Even when surrounded by peers or friends there was always a sense of impending desolation about Modest which made him clutch at those in his life a little too hard. This combined with his moodiness often eventually created the self-fulfilling prophecy of being alone, of which he had a reoccurring fear.

He probably would have been most happy with the sort of non-stop commune/squatter's party as Borodin had in his last years but Modest was not made the same way and such a thing would be impossible to sustain long term.

There was a distant, younger (25) cousin with whom he started to socialize. His cousin was a poet and inspired the melancholy melodies for "Bez Solnsta" and "Pesni Plyaski Smerti".

The rich subject matter of death started to enter his thoughts more frequently. His friend, the painter Victor Hartmann died. His watercolors inspire the cycle *Pictures at an Exhibit* which would later be orchestrated by Ravel (1922).

Once again, he would find himself alone partially from his drinking which brought on an even heavier depressive cycle of partaking. In isolation, he would begin to work on an opera which would be left unfinished.

Sorochynsti Fair was inspired by a Gogol story. Again, Modest would write the libretto himself. It was not a sense of foreboding which didn't allow for the opera's completion but his stop-start work habits.

Seeking further distraction outside the bottle, he undertook a tour of Southern Russia with the aged singer Darya Leonova. He thought it would earn them a lot of money. His peers worried about his reputation once he was away from home and those who put up with his moods because they knew him.

During the first leg of the tour it became apparent that they were not going to make the paydays which had been dreamed of. There was compensation found in the enthusiasm and excitement of the audiences and critics.

As the tour wore on the recitals were held in venues where they were no longer the sole act nor even necessarily the headliners. Their piano/singing duets became absorbed into a sort of variety show where music was interspersed with various short dramas, which often became the chief reason the audiences were in attendance.

Darya's singing still enthused the crowds but Modest went from receiving his own standing ovations as on the first part of the tour to more and more being pushed into the background as a mere accompanist.

There were surprisingly no explosive incidences but the luxury tour up the Volga river had to be sacrificed for a more direct and modest route home.

What he had wanted from the trip: money and lasting fame, did not occur but all the scenery which he had taken in greatly inspired him. During the final leg of the tour he came up with piano pieces which were programmatic improvisations, some of which unfortunately were never put to paper ("Storm on the Black Sea").   Ideas for more national pieces came to his mind along with other projects such as work based off text of Goethe and Pushkin.

There was no acrimonious break with Darya, he would dedicate several pieces to her after the tour. They would remain close but without the illusion of what touring in Russia could achieve. Briefly the thought of touring major cities in Europe was floated but Modest didn't have the physical stamina and his finances were a mess. Quietly, the idea was put to rest.

There was a period of several weeks in which no one heard from Modest as he worked in-between drinking. He was let go from his government job and groups of friends started two separate subscriptions to pay for him to finish   *Khovanshchina* and *Sorochynsti Fair*, neither of which he was able to finish.

Throughout his life Modest would often disappear for days, sometimes weeks on end only to eventually show up on a friend's doorstep ill. This dependence was a way of keeping people close to him, forcing upon them the need to nurse him back to health as to at the very least be able to get him once again out the door. His landlord kicked him out for nonpayment of rent and he ended up on the doorstep of a friend who, despite the inconvenience, took him in. While a houseguest he suffered three epileptic attacks which had been brought on from binge drinking. His friend found him a hospital to take him in.

While in the hospital he tried to behave but his body was already shot from years of abuse. He briefly rallied, posing for the famous painting by Ilya Repin (1844-1930) which has become the public's familiar image of him, red nosed, green jacketed with eyes which seem to reflect both mirth and world weariness at the same time. Shortly before his release he had taken to bribing an orderly to bring him bottles of cognac.

Getting out of the hospital he once again tried to temper his drinking but it was too late. Even if he had truly wanted to change, his body was spent. A month after being released from hospital he would die at the age of forty-two.

Out of all The Mighty Handful, Modest was the only one to grow up in the country. He was very influenced by the land, the ambient sounds of the serfs singing and talking. All the Mighty Handful wanted to represent Russia in their works but they would transmute it more than Modest. Of his first flush of compositions, the one which best showed what he would become and his link to the land was "Intermezzo Modo Classico" which was a programmatic piece describing peasants sinking into the snowbanks as they walk the Russian winter. From this piece on, he would be the least derivative composer of The Mighty Handful.

The span of his career was so brief that his work cannot be broken up into phases with clear lines of division as with so many other composers. It evolved rapidly with at least three major changes in style and some experiments too.

He learned composition by doing. Initially he worked mainly in short forms such as song. His work was nationalistic, programmatic and unorthodox in its harmonies and tonalities, which gave him no artistic predecessors. What makes his work's aesthetics so special is the sense of painterly poetics they offer to the listener.

Rather than his instrumental works, his artistic power can best be viewed through his work for voice. There managed to be a rich drama organically conveyed in his songs. The poetics of his songs, were more often than not, less academic and more about things that even the humblest of Russians experienced such as faith, death and love. Gustav Mahler's powerful song cycle on the death of children "Kindertotenlieder" (1901-04) was predated by Modest's own "Songs and dances of Death" (1877).

There were two things which for decades hindered his reputation and the true appreciation of his work. Some of his style was initially viewed as flawed and rife with mistakes by his friends and peers. This was especially considered true of his harmonies. A disservice too was the perpetuated myth of him being a type of modern primitive artistically. He was an intellectual and knowledgeable about contemporary aesthetic philosophies.

His knowledge was something which would cause him to freeze up in contemplation. This contributed to his slowing down production and ultimately along with other factors, the size of his oeuvre.

Initially after his death, fellow Mighty Handful member Rimsky Korsakov tried to "clean up" his scores for publication. When his works were corrected and made more orthodox, it robbed them of their power and distinctive identity, akin to an exotic animal now seen after being shot and taxidermized in a museum.

Years later, it was finally found that his unorthodoxy was part of his artistic identity and power. In 1928 the collected edition of his work as he wrote it was put out by Paul Lamm. Steadily, the music as was initially written has been replacing the corrected versions.

His works can be seen to be well outside of the two-main musical camps which largely at this time fell into Italian or German styles. The other members of his group helped contribute to the crucible of a new musical genre but they, like the original progenitor Glinka, still utilized discernable components from France and Italy. Through his deep affection for the land and its people, Modest Mussorgsky helped in creating a new genre of music. His personal style, so distinctive, sidestepped relying upon deriving its power from the shock of the new. It offers a timeless poetry which still possesses the power to move.

Nikolay Rimsky-Korsakov (1844-1908) is the best known of The Mighty Handful to the more casual music fan. His influence was different than that of his peers as it went beyond programmatic theory and inspiration. Eventually he would see the genre he helped create morph to become a hybrid of poetic melancholy which was often mixed with (exotic) orientalism. This seemed to not bother him at all as like the first conception of the genre, he was one of its chief progenitors, remaining for the later one of its best examples.

He was born into an aristocratic family. As a child, his chief two passions were music and the sea. His father would play musical games with him when he was only three years old. He would play a toy drum accompanying his father's piano playing. The tempo and rhythm would be changed without warning and he would keep in synch with his percussion. His mother also fostered his interest in music by singing to him often. These combined with an important early memory of a favorite uncle who sang him folk songs nurtured a deep-rooted appreciation for music.

When just eight years old he started piano lessons. At the age of nine he began to compose his own music without any kind of technical foundations. He attended a performance of Glinka's *A Life for the Tsar* which so moved and excited him that he began to attend other operatic performances. He considered Glinka's *Ruslan and Lyudmilia* "The best opera in the world". In this early phase of his musical life he was also enthusiastic about two foreign operas;

Lucia di Lammermoor and *Der Freischutz*.

All the men in his family had naval careers. The branches of his family tree included some admirals. Rimsky-Korsakov devoured books about the sea including ones on nautical terms. Model ships were built to give an even deeper understanding of the physicality of ships.

His brother, who was some twenty years older had him enroll in the Russian Imperial Naval College in St. Petersburg.

Rimsky-Korsakov maintained his passion for music even while pursuing his naval one. He taught himself composition by buying piano scores of Glinka's works and orchestrating and transcribing them. He also started a choral group at school, leading it in parts from Glinka's operas. As important a place as music had in his life, there was no thought given to pursuing it professionally.

When just seventeen, he met Balakirev (1861). As he did with anyone in whom he sensed potential, Balakirev proselytized his new artform. Rimsky-Korsakov's enthusiasm for Glinka served as the perfect entrée into Balakirev's circle. He was invited to attend Saturday night meetings of The Mighty Handful.

From Balakirev came the introduction to the music of Beethoven and Liszt. Both Western composers were important to the Handful for innovations in putting the conveying of sensations into music and programmatic possibilities. It was also felt that Liszt's philosophy incorporated some of that which they were trying to achieve, letting the materials (subject) dictate form instead of the usual of form dictating.

Liszt especially held importance for the group as he had known Glinka. Liszt's own work, even when not formally programmatic, sought to induce some type of emotional response. He had always been very supportive of new types of music. Having toured Russia several times, made his support seem less abstract.

Rimsky-Korsakov's interaction with the other members of the group deepened his appreciation of Russian philosophy and literature.

Part of the requirement for Rimsky-Korsakov's naval career was to do a world tour for three years (1862). His ship *The Almaz* made it as far afield as America in 1864. During his journey, he corresponded with Balakirev but outside of Russia, his musical life seemed almost a pleasant hobby.

He returned to Russia in 1865. His return posting ended up being St. Petersburg. This brought him back into direct contact with the group.

Once again taking up the Saturday night meetings while also going over his first symphony with Balakirev made him shed his passivity about viewing himself as a composer.

A serious study was made of piano. Once his renewed studies and interest in composing were underway he also returned to finishing his first symphony.

Balakirev was the director and chief conductor for the Free Music School of St. Petersburg. He premiered the symphony on a program comprised of the burgeoning nationalist genre.

Cui called it "The first Russian symphony." Present at the concert, the composer was called to the stage to receive an ovation, which he did in full naval uniform.

Fueled by his symphony's reception, Rimsky-Korsakov continued composing. The tempo of his production was steadier and with more speed than that of his peers. He varied his output, including in his first mature phase an overture, a tone poem and another symphony ("Antar Symphony").

Balakirev premiered his symphonic poem *"Sadko"*, which was instantly popular and finds itself still in many symphony's' repertoires. All the members of The Might Handful still associated but with the aesthetical philosophy now fully articulated and put into practice and an increasing public awareness of the form, differences in temperament started to become an issue.

Balakirev's manner of helping could come across as needlessly rigid in adhering to the original artistic mission's "rules". With all the members still having their day jobs, it was easy to gripe about each other without terminal breaks happening.

Rimsky-Korsakov desired to undertake a national opera (1868). *The Maid of Pskov* was completed in 1872. It was an immediate success with extended performance dates called for due to its popularity.

With his growing fame, the government first granted him special dispensation of not having to wear his naval uniform and then upon his resigning his post a special civilian one, inspector of naval bands, was created for him.

Being autodidactic, he had always used the technique of finding his way when writing. His conducting chores for the newly formed post furthered his education via practical application of leading the bands.

He possessed no foundation in harmony and counterpoint. Regardless of these gaps in traditional compositional foundation, the director of St. Petersburg Conservatory asked him to become professor of composition and instrumentation.

Knowing his own technical limitations, he thought to pass on the honor. His peers convinced him to take the post.

While teaching he also took the basic classes himself without the least trace of embarrassment. He immersed himself deeply in technical books while also taking guidance and aid from his wife, Nadeja who was an excellent musician with a formal musical education. Stravinsky (1882-1971) who, along with Schoenberg (1874-1951), it could be said all modern classical sprang from and Prokofiev (1891-1951) one of the greatest Russian symphonists, were students.

Conducting came to him quicker than the rudiments of composing. In 1874, he became Balakirev's successor as director/conductor of the Free Music School. He would hold this position for the next seven years.

He garnered a reputation for his conducting. This brought him other prestigious jobs including assistant director of the Imperial Chapel (1882-94) and conductor/director of concerts initiated by the publisher Mitrofon-Belyayev.

Allies were dropping by the wayside. Balakirev began to become oddly superstitious which was seen as no less off putting than his previous increasingly pedantic manner of teaching and overseeing the group. Mussorgsky felt that Rimsky-Korsakov had betrayed the spirit of the group with his new leaning towards formalized education and that his initial programming was not made up entirely of compositions by the group.

Borodin seemed to be the only one in the group with no axe to grind supporting the evolution of their comrade.

Although he had no use for the increasingly erratic Balakirev, Rimsky-Korsakov never broke faith with the initial intents of the groups mission. He reiterated his commitment repeatedly throughout the years after the groups demise.

Two years were spent (1875-77) putting together a survey of *One Hundred Russian Folk Songs* as to provide an overview to the public of the best of the genre. He also edited the operas of his former groups artistic forefather, Glinka.

With all that he had learned and the reminder of what had initially inspired him now mixing in his head, he wrote two new operas which while technically forward thinking embraced the nationalist aesthetic.

He also programmed four concerts which emphasized the music of The Mighty Handful, including premiers of works by Borodin and Mussorgsky.

By 1887 Borodin and Mussorgsky had died. Balakirev had isolated himself from society to delve into a hodge-podge of mysticism.

Rimsky-Korsakov created a new group but without giving it a formal name, nor overly specific tenets. Just as Balakirev had initially had a non-composer play an integral role in forming The Mighty Handful, this new group had the important publisher Belaiev as their patron.

In 1904-5 Russia was in an ill-advised war with Japan. It was unpopular, especially among students. This combined with the general revolution which the Russian military defeat helped feed into. Rimsky-Korsakov was publicly sympathetic to the disaffected students and was fired for his troubles. To further illustrate his its displeasure, the government prohibited performance of his works for several months.

Glazunov and Liadov, both professors and active members of the new musical group quit in protest to his firing as did some three hundred students.

Backing down in the face of yet more negative public perception, the government reinstituted a new conservatory with Glazunov as director and Rimsky-Korsakov once again also teaching.

For the rest of his life there would be bouts of ill health which effected his production and desire to write new works. The malaise would always wear off and his arguably most famous opera, *The Golden Cockerel* (1907) was written right before his death. He had stayed true to mission even in this final piece. This work combined a Russian background in its libretto based off the folkloric text by Pushkin, with satire on the current monarchy.

Like all the members of his first group, he had wanted a nationalistic art. Through travel, study and exposure to foreign peers and audiences, the "authenticity" of sound became less a rigid concern.

"Orientalism" in the works of the first wave of Russian composers was a way to put forth eroticism, politics and other things censors did not usually approve. It also allowed unorthodox scales and timbers to be introduced into works where formally would be far more standardized templates. Starting with him and magnifying up until the second world war, Eastern exoticism as Russia was frequently envisioned to be artistically comprised of, became a tonal shorthand often added to the palette when painting aural pictures.

All of the Mighty Handful had been self-taught. As time went on, the anti-institute stance became far less important to the evolving Rimsky-Korsakov. With progression of his abilities he also viewed it as somewhat a limitation.

He lived long enough to see the start of the conservatory system in which he actively participated. With the increasing exposure in the west to Russian music, to some extent the exoticism would become a trap too, with its expected aspects to be found in the music.

Russian opera, especially pre-Rachmaninoff (1873-1943) had a beautiful fatalism found within its works, either libretto wise or its cadence. Post, exoticism would wrap itself around these melancholy poetics. In both cases, it did manage to free itself of the French and German influences and just as any food one eats in France is French food, so too can it be said of

Russian music.

To work for oneself, be your own boss, is perceived as freedom. This is never true. It is merely a trade in of one set of worries for another.

When it's your business then all the profit is yours but so is all the worry. There is never truly "time off" because of all that is constantly at stake.

This aspect of being a business owner has the strongest commonality with that of being a working artist.

To be successful; not necessarily in a monetary sense but in regard to constantly evolving, while also garnering chops takes much discipline.

It is counter to the life of an artist as imagined by others or as portrayed in the media but a set schedule is of the utmost importance.

When one knows where they will be and what they shall be doing at a specific hour, the energy which might have to be used to think of those things can instead be put directly towards creating.

In Paris, I do my visual work during the day as the lighting is better. I get up early with no irony, I put on Monk's *April in Paris* while the coffee brews.

She remains in bed, tossing and turning. Always being careful of the imaginary cats as consciousness gently tugs at her.

Coffee and some pain tartine, then I work for a few hours as the market sets up.

This morning I found myself up extra early. After two days of rain by way of compensation, the sun joined me offering her full visage even at this early hour.

She sat up in bed sipping the coffee, now grown luke warm from her slow rise between writing postcards to Maggie, Katie and all the other saints of Ireland.

I did good work and with the collaboration of the sun, ahead of schedule. We could do our marketing and a little bit of flaneurism before lunch.

A sensual lunch in Montparnasse as can only be obtained in lieu of money by being a regular somewhere. For us, it was always Monsieur Marc's.

It is not gluttony but fact, if you come in under two hours then you have done it wrong.

Despite excellent coffee and calvados, we still must walk off the meal. We do the Luxembourg, taking the usual main paths.

Up the stairs, she leans against the stone railing and strikes a pose. In her light gray skirt and sleeveless ochre top with its rolled collar she possesses a casual elegance.

Although we do not seek to live this way, were a soundtrack to kick in, it could easily be a scene from a movie.

She pulls a camera from her bag and hands it to me. Surprisingly, she is able to strike the same pose with the exact previous casualness of a moment before.

I put my bookbag down between my feet which squeeze it tight for security. Looking through the viewfinder, what is she now thinking?

No, she has not changed, it is the onset of clouds. I get the shot and hand her the camera, taking the spot she had been standing in.

The rain comes. I tell her to wait a minute.

In a moment, a bigger darker cloud will be upon us with a heavier rain emerging from its grayish sheen.

I look up, holding my hat in my hands against my chest.

"Come on, it's really starting to come down."

"OK, now, this is me, go ahead."

She has known me too long now to comment on my choices.

I still felt too full to go home. She thought it potentially merely an excuse to go poke around the record store. I told her that I was fine with her heading back and us meeting up later.

Percussive kiss on the cheek which smelled faintly of coffee and apples from Normandy and I was off.

I found a few interesting obscure things almost immediately and decided not to jinx future endeavors by continuing to look.

I walk home, taking all the little side streets of which I am the king. To travel the city in this way, brief little vignettes play out, framed by windows or wrought iron balconies with their window boxes of geraniums.

It is the reiteration that one is in the stream of life.

Today it occurs to me, all the hours that I spend alone, working, it is only the things done in solitude that go out into the world, connecting with and touching people whom I will never know.

ABOUT THE AUTHOR

Wayne H.W Wolfson is a multi-medium artist whose writing has appeared in many journals. His visual work has appeared in galleries, group shows and is in private collections worldwide.

www.ingramcontent.com/pod-product-compliance
Lightning Source LLC
Chambersburg PA
CBHW072137170526
45158CB00004BA/1405